MOUNTAIN BIKE GUIDE

East Midlands

D1197072

by

Dave Taylor

Published by The Ernest Press 1998
© Copyright Dave Taylor

ISBN 0 948153 58 X

A CIP catalogue record for this book is available from the
British Library, Wetherby

Front cover illus: Looking out from Burrough Hill (Note that the
bike has been pushed and not ridden as there is
no bridleway.)
Rear cover illus: Burrough Hill route

Typeset from the author's disk by Stanningley Serif
Printed by Colorcraft, Hong Kong

CONTENTS

Acknowledgements 5
Overview Map 6
Preface 7
Introduction 8
Key to Sketch-maps 18

The Routes

NOTTINGHAMSHIRE

Welbeck and Clumber 23
Sherwood Forest 29
The West Leake Hills 35

LEICESTERSHIRE

Charnwood Forest 41
Barkby 47
Tilton and Quenby 53
Burrough Hill 59
Launde Abbey 65
Twycross 71
Market Bosworth and the Ashby Canal 77
Leicester Forest 83
Rolleston 89
Medbourne 97
Foxton Locks 103

NORTHAMPTONSHIRE

Fineshade and King's Cliffe 109
Lyveden New Bield 115
Cottesbrooke 119
Canons Abbey 125
Silverstone 131

WARWICKSHIRE

Brinklow 137
The Priors 143

THE LEICESTERSHIRE BIKE ROUND 149

ACKNOWLEDGEMENTS

This guide would not have been completed without the help and support of my wife, Carol. Without her encouragement the book would probably have sunk without trace — most likely in an extremely muddy field somewhere in Northamptonshire! I thank my wife also for being general navigator, support vehicle driver, photographer on occasions and most importantly of all, my companion on many of the routes. She also makes the best home-made soup in the world — just what you need after a hard day in the saddle!

I am also most grateful to Mr Frisby of Elms Farm, Appleby Parva for allowing use of a section of private track from reference SK 30550735 to 30800750. This is not a public right of way and the use of it or the inclusion of it in this book does not imply such.

I would also like to thank all those helpful people at the various county councils whom I have pestered on occasions in my efforts to ensure that the routes contained within this book are legal. In particular Peter Jarman, Rural Cycling Officer for Nottinghamshire County Council for his help and advice concerning on and off-road routes in Nottinghamshire, Mr B Robinson of the Department of Planning and Transportation at Leicestershire County Council and Mr P Williams, Definitive Map Officer, and his colleagues at Warwickshire County Council for their continuing help in sorting out a little problem! Also Mr Peter Brett, Manager for Northants Forest District, for clarifying the situation regarding cycling in Fineshade Wood.

I would also like to thank Jeremy Bass, a colleague of mine, for his expert help and tuition in using the computer to draw the route maps, and his general advice on matters concerning computer graphics.

Lastly, thanks to all those mountain bikers I met whilst out doing these routes. Their friendliness and enthusiasm helped provide me with the inspiration to complete this guide.

The East Midlands

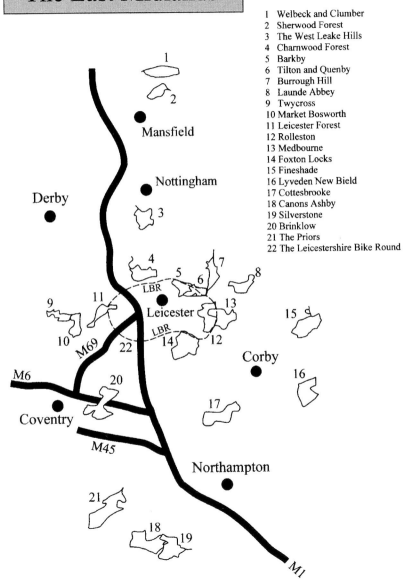

1 Welbeck and Clumber
2 Sherwood Forest
3 The West Leake Hills
4 Charnwood Forest
5 Barkby
6 Tilton and Quenby
7 Burrough Hill
8 Launde Abbey
9 Twycross
10 Market Bosworth
11 Leicester Forest
12 Rolleston
13 Medbourne
14 Foxton Locks
15 Fineshade
16 Lyveden New Bield
17 Cottesbrooke
18 Canons Ashby
19 Silverstone
20 Brinklow
21 The Priors
22 The Leicestershire Bike Round

PREFACE

Since producing the previous version of this book, *Mountain Bike Guide: The Midlands*, it became clear that some alterations needed to be made in the rewrite. In making these changes I have endeavoured in various ways to produce an even better guide.

Firstly, the original guide covered a very wide area, perhaps an unconscious ploy to make it appeal to a large number of people. However, it became clear whilst researching that there were many more routes to be discovered. As a consequence, I decided to split the book into two parts. This book, the first, covers the East Midlands area including as far north as Sherwood Forest, south to Silverstone in Northamptonshire, and everything east of Coventry over towards Rutland. The extensive motorway network makes access to the routes in this guide very quick and easy. The second book for the West Midlands will follow.

Secondly, I have long held the idea of an off-road route encircling Leicester, which is in the centre of the area covered by the guide. A footpath route, 'The Leicestershire Round', has been in existence for many years and it became apparent, during researching for new routes, that it would be possible to link many of the routes in the new guide to produce one mega-route wending its way through the often very pretty countryside that surrounds Leicester. I therefore present my version of 'The Leicestershire Bike Round', a route of approximately 120 km, linked together via bridleways, by-ways, & unclassified county roads with a minimum of main roads. I am sure that others can make improvements and I look forward to hearing of any ideas, via the publishers.

Thirdly, it will be apparent from the East Midlands area map that many of the routes lie close to each other and therefore the possibility of linking them exists. Where possible I have indicated, on the maps and/or in the text, how these routes might be linked so as to produce even longer routes, in the hope of satisfying those committed masochistic, mud-plodders!

Fourthly, it will be clear from the original guide that my map-drawing abilities are somewhat limited. I have attempted to rectify this problem, with the aid of new technology, and I hope that the new maps are easier to follow.

INTRODUCTION

At first sight, it might appear that a book entitled *Mountain Bike Guide: The East Midlands* could be a contradiction in terms. True, although there are few mountains in the Midlands, there are many hills and the area is criss-crossed by a network of ancient tracks, bridleways, dis-used county roads, canals and pretty country lanes. All of these, when carefully linked together, make for very interesting and enjoyable on and off-road biking.

Recent years have seen an explosion in the popularity of moun-tain biking, if retail sales of bikes are any indication. In reality the author suspects that although many mountain bikes are sold each year, a significant number rarely, if ever, see a grassy bridleway, woodland track or rocky hill path! Where mountain bikes are used off-road in appreciable numbers, such as in areas like the Lake District or the Dales, they are perceived as yet another threat to an already over-stressed environment. One of the aims of this book is to redress the balance somewhat. This guide illustrates that there is plenty of moun-tain biking fun to be had in other areas of the country, which can be just as challenging in its own right.

Many owners of mountain bikes, particularly those new to the sport, do not necessarily relish the challenge of carrying a bike to the top of a 3000ft mountain, but would appreciate simple, easy to fol-low and reliable descriptions of where to ride off-road, legally. This book will provide some guidance for such folk, although it would be a mistake to assume that all the routes in this book are easy! In any case, given the wrong conditions even the easiest looking route can become a real challenge.

The routes described vary greatly in style and difficulty. Some would make an ideal day out for a family group, whilst the more experienced hammerhead might prefer to thrash around in an afternoon. Other routes are perhaps best savoured on a fine summers evening, when there are fewer people about and the pubs are more likely to be open. Whatever type of mountain biker you are, I am sure that you'll find that these routes will prove interesting and enjoyable. Mountain biking should not only be about having the latest bits of high-tech gear, but also about appreciating the countryside, with a little bit of fitness and a lot of fun.

ENVIRONMENT

One of my concerns as the author of this guide, has been its potential effect on the environment. Fortunately, unlike the more popular areas such as the Lake District, there is not yet generally perceived to be a great problem with mountain bikes in the Midlands. Whilst it is the intention to encourage mountain biking in the area, it is hoped that this guide will not create problems of conflict of interest.

In spite of the fact that the area contains such large conurbations as Nottingham, Leicester and Coventry, the rural districts between are very quiet and, as yet, largely unexplored by mountain bikers. Roadies have long been aware of the potential for riding in this area, on quiet lanes which are largely deserted of major traffic even on a Sunday afternoon.

True, it would be misleading to suggest that it is possible to devise completely off-road routes in the area, but by linking bridleways and tracks with small country lanes it is easy to create interesting routes. Herein, however, lies a slight problem. The area is characterised by quite intensive farming and although bridleways may exist on the Ordnance Survey map, the reality can be different on the ground. The continued existence of a bridleway seems to depend to a great extent on whether or not there is a history of horse riding in the area. Where the latter is the case, the bridleway may well have been downgraded to a footpath or lost altogether. This situation has, however, improved in recent years as many county councils struggle to record and clarify the rights of way in their area prior to the year 2000. Even where the bridleway still exists, the amount of use that it gets determines whether it is possible to ride it or not. Whatever the case, the continued use of such bridleways by mountain bikers will only be accepted by local farmers and the public if they can be persuaded that mountain bikers are essentially jolly decent, country loving folk, at least in public!

Unfortunately, even with the best intentions, conflicts do arise. Since producing the original version of the guide a few problems have come to the author's notice. To illustrate this point I take the particular case of a bridleway which runs to Heathcote Farm near Wellesbourne in Warwickshire. This route was in the original Midlands, but as you will see, not in the new East Midlands guide book. The author was under the impression that the bridleway continued past the farm house, but this is apparently not the case. The problem would not have been so great, but for the poor attitude of some groups of mountain bikers towards the farmer, whose land they were crossing. This has not helped the image of mountain bikers and it has certainly not increased access to the countryside. As has been pointed out elsewhere in the book, the countryside is a place of work; it is where people earn their living, and if we are all to enjoy it we must work together.

The author has made every effort to ensure that the routes in this book use legal rights of way, but the existence of a route in the book is not proof that a right of way exists. There is no point in waving the book, or a photocopy of it, at an irate farmer, who has probably lived there all his life, if he thinks you should not be there. Just smile nicely and leave. Check the problem out with the County Council Rights of Way people if you feel you have a just cause.

The Twycross route, featured in this guide, is an example of how working together can improve access to the countryside. Mr Frisby, the farmer and landowner at Elms Farm, Appleby Magna, has kindly agreed that mountain bikers can use a stretch of track across his land. This section is not a right of way and is permissive only, but it links an unclassified road, Windmill Lane, to a bridleway, Salt Street. This also improves the quality of the route greatly and causes less disturbance to all concerned.

In essence, enjoy yourself in the country, but be considerate of others. If you follow the Off-Road and Country Codes, then you cannot go far wrong.

The Off Road Code
- Only ride where you know you have a legal right,
- Always give way to horses and pedestrians,
- Avoid animals and crops,
- Take all litter with you,
- Leave all gates as found,
- Keep the noise down,
- Don't get annoyed with anyone, it never solves problems,
- Always try to be self-sufficient, for you and your bike,
- Never create a fire hazard.

In addition to this there is of course the Country Code, issued by the Countryside Commission.

The Country Code
- Enjoy the countryside and respect its life and work,
- Guard against the risk of fire,
- Fasten all gates ,
- Keep your dogs under close control,
- Keep to public rights of way across farmland,
- Use gates (and stiles) to cross fences, hedges and walls,
- Leave livestock, crops and machinery alone,
- Take your litter home,
- Help keep all water clean,
- Protect wildlife, plants and trees,
- Take special care on country roads,
- Make no unnecessary noise.

All of the above begs the question, what actually is a right of way?

RIGHTS OF WAY

The future of mountain biking is very much in the hands of those who ride mountain bikes. The whole ethos associated with mountain biking is one of fun, freedom and adventure. Although rules seem to be the antipathy of the sport, these codes need to be followed. It is very easy to be romantic about the rural landscape. In reality, particularly in the Midlands, the countryside is one big factory, albeit a very pretty one on occasions. Landowners and farmers who view the countryside as a business do not take kindly to the public, whether on foot, horse or bike, causing disruption and possibly threatening their livelihood. It is essential, therefore, to be aware of where you may ride legally.

There are four types of right of way as detailed on the OS maps, of which three are open to off-road riding.

Public Footpath — this is a right of way on foot only. Mountain bikers do not have a right of way on footpaths. If you ride your bike onto a footpath you are committing a civil offence and as such could be sued by the landowner for damage to property. On a more practical note, footpaths will usually have a stile at each field boundary and, after trying to carry your bike over these a few times, you will begin to wonder whether it is worth it. Best advice is, keep off — no go area.

Bridleways — These are open to the public on foot, on horseback and on bicycle, provided that cyclists give way to horses and pedestrians. It is important to remember that cyclists have only had this right since 1968 and are therefore comparative newcomers, so smile nicely and give way to any walkers or horses that you see. Bridleways are usually marked by a blue waymarker, although not all local councils are as careful as they might be and, occasionally, you may only see yellow footpath markers.

BOATS — or By-ways Open to All Traffic. As the classification implies, these are open to all vehicles as well as pedestrians, horses and cyclists. Unfortunately, a minority of users of four-wheel drive vehicles and motorcycles have succeeded in making a real mess of some of these excellent tracks and even the adjoining land, much to the annoyance of the landowners.

RUPPS — These are Roads Used as Public Paths. Take care with these! In the Midlands at least, these have a nasty habit of no longer existing on the ground, or have been downgraded to the status of a footpath. Where they do exist many local councils are now in the process of reclassifying these as BOATs or Bridleways.

In addition to the four types of rights of way there are also:

Unclassified County Roads — These very minor roads are often unsurfaced and are usually not maintained. Whilst not strictly 'off-road' as such, they can range in appearance from superb walled tracks to little more than linear depressions in the ground. In effect they have the same status as a by-way but on the map it may not be clear whether they are a right of way or a private track. Consultation with the definitive map held by the Highways department of the County Council will usually clarify.

UCRs are used quite extensively in this book and the reader will notice that on occasions these tracks may not appear even on the 1:50 000 OS maps. Have no fear: follow the route descriptions carefully — all of these tracks have been checked by the author with the relevant County Council Highways Departments.

Canal tow-paths — The industrial heritage of the Midlands has bequeathed an extensive network of canals and their associated tow-paths. With the increase in leisure activities in general, many of these tow-paths are now in excellent condition, but it is important to remember that these paths are not public rights of way. British Waterways, who own most of the canal network, do allow use of the tow-paths by cyclists, subject to certain restrictions. Firstly, in order to use the path it is necessary to obtain and subsequently display, a permit from British Waterways. The address is included in the appendix. Secondly, certain stretches of canal may not be available to cyclists due to, for example, the condition of the path or the tow-path coinciding with a public footpath. That said, the canal system is very extensive and whilst it may not present the most challenging off-road riding, it is often very scenic and is useful in linking more off-road sections together. Take care, however! Tow-paths can be rather narrow in places and soft at the edges. Look out for low bridges and obstructions on the path. Keep your speed down and be aware, otherwise you might just take an unexpected dip in the murky waters.

Forest Tracks — A great deal of woodland is managed by Forest Enterprise on behalf of the Forestry Commission. In the past, access has been difficult, but recently the Commission has shown a more enlightened attitude and opened up areas of their land for leisure activities, initially for walkers. All tracks on Forestry Commission land are private, unless they coincide with recognized rights of way. However, in many areas, the Commission have indicated that they are happy for bikers to use some of the gravel tracks within their forests, although this should always be checked with the local office, as restrictions may be introduced at any time.

If you do use the forestry tracks, have consideration for others. There is a strong urge to 'let rip' on these tracks and as a consequence terrify the local Sunday afternoon trippers! This is a sure way to get mountain bikers banned from the forest and has already created problems in certain areas. To alleviate problems of this nature, the Forestry Commission are now making available areas specifically aimed at mountain bikers. A good example of this is Sherwood Pines Forest in Nottinghamshire, which has waymarked trails of varying difficulty. Facilities of this kind can be expected only if mountain bikers show that they are responsible users of the countryside.

EQUIPMENT

Although this guide shows that it is perfectly possible to bike off-road in the Midlands and escape the hassle of modern life, an off-road experience in Northamptonshire is hardly likely to have the same degree of seriousness as a day out on Helvellyn. There are, however, a few points about equipment that are relevant, regardless of where you are biking.

The Bike

The type of mountain bike you prefer to ride is very much a personal choice. There is a great deal of hype surrounding mountain biking technology that, for most people, is pretty irrelevant, except when it comes to 'pose value'! Choose the best bike you can afford, but remember what you are going to put it through. A well built chromoly bike may be a more sensible choice than the latest aluminium and titanium technology, bedecked with numerous widgets. That said, there are a few devices that I have found particularly helpful when biking in the Midlands. As you might expect, mud can be more than a slight problem in this part of the country! Personally, I detest mud guards, but I have found the detachable Crud Catcher an excellent insurance against those unpleasant 'black outs' caused by flying mud from the front wheel when on a rapid descent. An equally useful device is the Crud Claw, which is excellent at scraping mud and bits of arable field out of the rear mech.

Clothing and Safety

Again, this is a very personal matter and there is more than enough advice in the magazines and books on what should be worn. In the event of a crash, however, what you are wearing could have an important effect on how well you survive! One item that is essential, is a helmet. Find one that fits well and use it! This may seem a pain at first, and helmets are not cheap, but consider the consequences of a bad crash without one. Having seen how effective they are in practice, I have no doubt about their value. Also, consider investing in a pair of gloves, they will make the ride more comfortable and protect your hands in the event of a fall. Glasses too, are a good idea. Not only do they look cool, they also keep nasties like bugs, mud and twigs out of your eyes. Whilst on the subject of safety, it is perhaps a good idea to carry a small first-aid kit. This might include nothing more than a few plasters, a roll of bandage, lint, and a pair of scissors, but you never know when it might be needed!

Tools

Many books have been written regarding the maintenance and repair of bikes and I would not presume to improve on their advice. A basic tool kit can, however, prevent a pleasant day out from degenerating into farce. At a minimum the kit should include — a universal spanner, Allen keys, small screwdriver, tyre levers, pump, spare tube and puncture repair kit. The last three items I have found absolutely essential. A particular problem in the Midlands is the prevalence of hedges (particularly alongside canals) which, after they have been trimmed, leave nice little sharp thorns all over the track. Expect puncture repairs to be the norm!

THE ROUTES

Each route is accompanied by a map, a summary, details of the route, an introduction and a description. I have tried to indicate places of interest *en route* within the introduction and occasionally in the description. A few words of explanation are required regarding the route details.

Grade — I have found it particularly difficult to grade these routes. A descriptive grade can only be subjective at the best of times and is always dependant on many factors. In trying to grade these routes I have assumed that the rider is of very average fitness, that is, they are neither a couch potato nor a health and fitness freak given to 100km bike rides. I have also assumed that the surface conditions are reasonably good, i.e. not completely waterlogged. The ridability of some of the routes is severely affected by the surface conditions. In very wet conditions it becomes impossible even to push a bike across ploughed fields, let alone ride it. I have assumed a fairly typical (?) British summer of sunshine and showers, hence you should expect quite boggy bits in the woods. Less than ideal conditions could increase the difficulty considerably. The grades are also specific to the East Midlands. Assuming good surface conditions, many of these routes would probably be graded as easy or moderate on a national basis, if only because the hills are of modest size. This would be of little help and could be misleading, as the difficulty of these routes is frequently dependent upon the state of the ground.

I have therefore used a subjective system of grading similar to that used in rock climbing. Each grade is severely affected by personal fitness, surface conditions and should be taken with a large bucket of salt!

Easy — Few difficulties, probably uses canal tow-paths and a reasonable proportion of country lanes, only crosses fields on good tracks, little or no hill climbing.

Moderate — Some slight difficulties may be encountered, perhaps due to soft woodland tracks and occasional poor field-edge bridleways.

Difficult — Expect difficulties with bridleways across arable fields and/or soft woodland tracks. Some hill climbs.

Very difficult — Definitely has sections of soft woodland tracks and across arable fields on ill-defined tracks. Expect (and enjoy) hill climbs.

Severe — totally flat countryside, non-existent tracks across ploughed fields, after a month of torrential rain. Fortunately, there are no such routes in this guide!

----------	Bridleway, usually a single track.
==========	Bridleway, BOAT, RUPP, UCR.
	Metalled road.
	Stream or river.
	Trees.
PH	Public house.
	Bridge.
◢	Buildings.
✝	Church.
✕	Battlefield site.
✛	Deserted village.
200 △	Trig point and height in metres.
	Windmill.
	Site of ancient fort or castle.

Time — The times can only be approximate, bearing in mind the factors described above. I have not allowed any time for cream teas, quick pints, jam butties, photos or puncture repairs!

Distance — I have tried to indicate the approximate proportion of on and off-road riding. A minimum requirement when researching the routes was that each route should be at least 50% off-road. A second requirement was that any road riding should be on as few class A or B roads as possible. The vast majority of the roads used in these routes are in fact small, little used country lanes, with only the occasional use of a B road and, rarely, an A road.

MAPS
As will be evident from the sketch-maps for each route, I am, by no stretch of the imagination, an expert cartographer. Each map is intended only as guidance to support the route description. I would strongly recommend that the relevant Ordnance Survey map for the area be referred to for more information.

The best map to use (aside from the 1:10 000 definitive maps held by the County Councils) is the Pathfinder 1:25 000 series. Unfortunately, the area covered by this guide is so large that the cost of buying all the required Pathfinders would be prohibitive! However, armed with this guide book and the relevant 1:50 000 Landranger maps, you should encounter no route finding problems. The complete list of required maps is as follows,

120 Mansfield, Worksop & surrounding area
129 Nottingham and Loughborough
140 Leicester & Coventry
141 Kettering, Corby & surrounding area
151 Stratford-upon-Avon & surrounding area
152 Northampton & Milton Keynes area

LINKING ROUTES
Although some of the routes detailed in this guide are of fairly

modest length, it is quite possible to combine routes to produce more demanding excursions which might appeal to the more committed biker. As I have indicated in the route descriptions, it is easily possible to combine the Welbeck and Clumber route with that of the Sherwood Forest. Alternatively, to the west of Leicester, the Twycross and Market Bosworth routes may be combined, and even linked to the Leicester Forest route.

Combining routes is especially possible with the routes in East Leicestershire, where there is a wealth of old unclassified county roads and bridleways. For example, it is quite feasible to combine the Barkby route with Tilton and Quenby. Alternatively, the Burrough Hill route can be combined with Rolleston and Quenby. Starting at Melton Mowbray, follow the Burrough route to Tilton on the Hill, then take the small lanes and field roads via Skeffington to Rolleston. Here follow the Rolleston route, returning via Rolleston and a green lane to Billesdon, and then on to the Quenby route. Continue around this to Marefield and return to Melton Mowbray as per the Burrough Hill route.

In fact the permutations and combinations to the east of Leicester are so numerous that it is difficult to know how not to produce a new version of a route. Perhaps the ultimate in linking routes is my newly created Leicestershire Bike Round. This uses sections of Leicester Forest, Barkby, Rolleston, Foxton Locks and many other bits of off-road that I never quite found time to turn into routes in their own right. And this is the fun part about it. There are many routes out there waiting to be found, so go out and explore!

Busaco Cliffs, Welbeck

Welbeck and Clumber

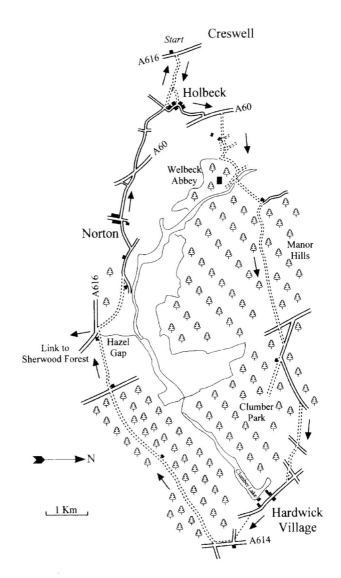

Welbeck and Clumber

Route Summary
Creswell, Holbeck, Welbeck Park, Robin Hood Way, Clumber Park, Hardwick Village, Duncanwood, Hazel Gap, Norton, Holbeck, Creswell.

Details
Grade — Moderate
Time — 3 1/2 hours
Distance — 29 km: off road — 21 km
                   on road — 8 km
Terrain — Mostly flat with a few gentle hills
Surface—- Excellent green lanes and gravel forest tracks
Start Grid Reference — SK 532 734
Maps — Mansfield, Worksop & surrounding area L120, Sherwood
       Forest Explorer 28.

Introduction
The area of Nottinghamshire to the north-east of Mansfield has many exciting off-road possibilities. Clumber Park is well known for its forest tracks, which are much used by cyclists and mountain bikers. This route starts just south of the village of Creswell, famous for its Crags which are well worth a visit. The route also passes Welbeck Abbey, the seat of the Dukes of Portland. Apparently, the fifth Duke was of such a retiring nature that he shut himself off from the rest of the world. In order that he would not be seen he indulged in building extravagant underground constructions, including a huge ballroom and also many inter-connecting tunnels used for racing his horses. You can still see the remains of these as you cross the estate, for example in White Deer Park.

   The route continues on through to Clumber Park and down to Hardwick, an estate village now the centre of administration for the National Trust who manage the Park. The National Trust have recognised the interest in cycling and have a number of family routes marked out in the area. Our route makes its way back through some excellent woods and finally via Holbeck, back to the start. For those of a more adventurous nature it is possible to link this route to the Sherwood Forest route further south, for example at Hazel Gap.

Route Description

Start at about 1 km south of **Creswell** on the A616, where there is a bridleway. Follow the excellent green lane down, then up to arrive eventually at a road. Go left and into the village of **Holbeck**. After leaving the village the road bears left and then does a sharp right taking you onto to the main A 60. Turn left onto the road and after only half a kilometre, turn right where it is signed the Welbeck Estate. Follow this estate road, which is also a bridleway, until you arrive at a lodge. Continue straight on where there is a bridleway sign, across an arable field. Follow the estate road round towards some woods and at the woods turn left where there is a bridleway sign. The green lane passes along the edge of the woods and down to another estate road. Turn right here and into the woods. Bear left, follow the road around and then sharp left, where there is a bridleway sign. This can easily be missed in a rush, so don't continue straight on where it says 'Private No Entry' — they do not take kindly to unwanted visitors! After going left the track passes between the lakes and there is a good view of Gouldsmeadow Lake on your left. Follow the well-defined track out of the woods and across arable fields towards the forest. This track crosses White Deer Park and follows one of Welbeck's famous tunnels.

Soon you arrive at South Lodge. Go straight ahead and through a couple of bridle gates, past the lodge and some chickens, and then turn right. The bridleway now takes you into the woods. The track climbs steadily through the woods and then, at Busaco Crags, enters a little gorge. Generations of visitors have carved their initials in the sandstone rock and the place has a real atmospheric feel about it. One can easily imagine Robin Hood and his Merry Men leaping from the

Clumber Lake

crags and demanding that you hand over your valuables immediately! So hang on to them tight and continue down what is called Drinking Pit Lane, which is a real pleasure to ride. Too soon it arrives at a road which you cross over. Continue along another forestry track, soon to meet another road. Go right here and towards Truman's Lodge, an entrance to **Clumber Park**. Bear left before the lodge and follow the road. After about a kilometre take the second bridleway on your right and enter the forest. This track takes you through the forest and to a road, which is called Limetree Avenue (for reasons that will be apparent). Cross over and to your left you will see a bridleway sign. Follow the track along the edge of a conifer plantation, but look out for a bridleway sign pointing left. Follow this up through the trees, across a forestry road, through more trees and finally to another road, where you go right.

This forestry road takes you down to the village of **Hardwick**. This picturesque estate village is the administrative centre of Clumber Park. Stop off at the carpark and take a look at Clumber Lake. You also stand a good chance of an ice cream here as well. Biking is allowed around the lake and the National Trust have a number of family bike routes for the area. Continue out of the village and across the ford over the River Poulter. This is an excellent wildlife spot where you will see many birds and hear sedge warblers and blackcaps. Take care over the ford as it can be slippery. Follow the road and after a couple of hundred metres, bear left through a wide gap in the hedge and follow a well-defined path which cuts diagonally across an arable field towards some trees. This bridleway takes you past the trees and down to an entrance to Clumber Park on the **A614**. Originally the route was to continue down the main road, but the National Trust have been very kind and constructed a cycle track which runs parallel with the road. Cross over the drive and follow the cycleway down through trees, over another drive and into the woods.

After c.400 metres you meet the bridleway proper, called Freeboard Lane. Look out for the old picnic table and then turn right. At the time of writing the bridleway was a delightful little track that wound its way through dense woodland, though with the improvements going on, that may not be the case for much longer. Follow the bridleway past South Lodge and eventually you arrive at the carpark at Duncan Wood. Cross over the road and continue along a fenced off track which follows the edge of a field. This is in fact a RUPP. The track becomes narrower then, joins a wider forestry track. Soon you come to **Hazel Gap** carpark and you can, if you want, link to the Sherwood Forest route further south. Our route crosses the carpark and then continues NW down a wooded green lane. The lane rollercoasters its way through woods and past fields, eventually arriving at **Corunna Lodge** and a road.

At the road, go straight on (left) and past Bentinck Lodge. Look out for the memorial which was erected in memory of Lord George Bentinck, a son of the fourth Duke of Portland, who died near here whilst out on a walk. Follow the road round left and into the village of **Norton**. The road bears left in the village and then you take the first, immediate right. Follow the lane up to the A60, which you cross with care. Continue along Elma Lane for **Holbeck**, until you arrive at a staggered crossroads. Continue straight on and up a narrower and mossy lane to a T-junction at the top. Cross straight over and return to the start via the green lane that you started out on.

Sherwood Forest

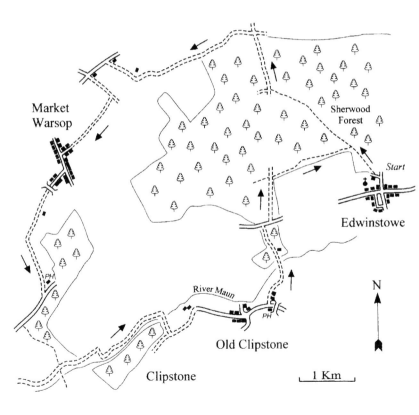

Sherwood Forest

Route Summary
Edwinstowe, Sherwood Forest, Market Warsop, Redbrick House, Maun Valley, Old Clipstone, Sherwood Forest, Edwinstowe.

Details
Grade — moderate
Time — 2 1/2 hrs
Distance — 24 km: off road — 20 km
                                on road — 4 km
Terrain — Mostly level but with a few hills.
Surface — Excellent forestry tracks and solid bridleways
Start Grid Reference — SK 625672
Maps — Mansfield, Worksop & surrounding area L120, Sherwood
         Forest Explorer 28.

Introduction
Sherwood Forest lies just to the north-east of Mansfield and is surrounded by the remnants of its industrial past and present. Even so, there are many excellent bridleways that wend their way through largely unspoilt countryside. The route starts at Edwinstowe and follows the bridleway towards Gleadthorpe. There is a temptation here to explore the forest, but bikes are strictly limited to the bridleways.

After leaving the forest the route passes through Market Warsop (as quickly as possible!) and on to the Maun Valley. This secluded valley, so close to human habitation, is a wildlife sanctuary. The route continues through Old Clipstone, crosses the valley again, and then climbs up past Archway House. This curious building, now a private house, was once a hunting lodge and was built by the fourth Duke of Portland in 1844. The lodge is an imitation of the gatehouse at Worksop Priory, but instead of having statues of saints in its niches, it is bedecked with statues of Robin Hood and his Merry Men.

The route returns to the start via Sherwood Forest. If time allows

Archway House, Maun Valley

you can visit the Major Oak, where Robin Hood is alleged to have hidden, and the visitors centre for refreshments.

A possible extension to the route, or even just for its own sake, could involve a detour at Old Clipstone to the Clipstone Forest, or Sherwood Pines Forest Park as it is otherwise known. Off-road biking is encouraged here and there is a bike hire shop at the visitors centre. Always check out access on the day, however, as sections might be closed off for forestry operations.

Route Description

The route starts at the Sherwood Forest carpark just outside the village of Edwinstowe. Follow the bridleway which goes north-west along the edge of the open park land and is signed for Gleadthorpe. You soon enter the forest and the way is marked by little horseshoe bridleway markers, but watch out as they can be hidden in the undergrowth and we wouldn't want to get lost would we? The excellent track makes its way through pleasant mixed woodland and after a while narrows to a delightful single track. Eventually you come to a wide forestry road, where you bear right (N). Follow the main track downhill slightly (a bridleway sign) and along the edge of the forest with **Budby South Forest** clearing on your right. After about a kilometre you come to a forestry cross-roads and you go left. The route descends, crosses over another track and then climbs uphill slightly. Where the main track bears left you continue straight on (right). Continue on where there is a bridleway sign and along the edge of the wood. The narrow track does lots of fun twists and turns and eventually comes to the end of the wood. Continue on along the right-hand edge of the field on a reasonable track, soon to join a green lane which descends. At a cross-roads of tracks, carry straight on and down Broomhill Lane. This takes you past a sewage works (how delightful!) and over a bridge and down to a small lane.

Bear left at the lane and just past **Burns Farm** you will see a bridleway on your left. Go through the gate, up a narrow lane and then join a good farm track. Follow this and, shortly after going under a railway bridge, you will see a bridleway sign on your right. This takes you along another green lane but, where this bears left, you continue straight on and along the edge of a field. The track is well defined and eventually takes you back over the railway line and into the outskirts of **Market Warsop**. This next section is probably not the most beautiful part of the route, but then it will only serve to enhance the rest! Trying to look real cool, hurtle down to the main B6035 and go left. Take the second right along Oakfield Lane and after passing some houses, a railway bridge and a waste disposal site (lovely!) you finally escape into the Nottinghamshire countryside again.

The lane becomes a wide sand and gravel track which climbs gently towards and then goes along the side of some woods. You arrive at the main A6075 by the Redbrick House Hotel, where you go right. After less than a kilometre you will see a layby on your left and a bridleway. Follow the bridleway down the edge of the wood, continuing straight on (right) where there is a sign indicating that you are on the Maun Valley Trail. The delightful track descends by the edge of the wood and wends its way through a nature reserve rich in bracken, broom and wild flowers. Too soon you leave the woods and continue on down the edge of a meadow, through a small copse and arrive at a junction of bridleways. Turn left and follow the sandy track which eventually turns right and goes down to the bottom of the valley by the **River Maun**. The track goes sharp left and then follows alongside the river and with a series of pools on your left. This is a favourite spot for fishing so watch out for wayward rods and lines. After about a kilometre the track comes to a caravan site and you turn right, go over the river via a bridge, and climb up into the woods. Where the track forks you bear right and soon arrive at a bridleway which runs along the edge of the wood. Go left here and follow the track past the riding stables at Cavendish Lodge, then onto tarmac and down Squires Lane and into **Old Clipstone**.

At the T-junction in the village go right and up to the main B6030 where you go left for Ollerton. Follow the main road round

On the Maun Valley Way

for only a short distance until you see a bridleway on your left, just before and opposite the Dog and Duck pub (time for refreshments?). Follow the bridleway, which bears right, goes under a railway bridge and then left under a second bridge. This is Clipstone Junction. The track takes you down to Forge Bridge over the River Maun and then climbs up towards some woods. As you enter the woods you will see the rather incongruous Archway House ahead, once used as a hunting lodge, but now a private house. Continue on past (look out for the Robin Hood figures) and at the main A6075, go right. After only a couple of hundred metres you will see a bridleway sign on the left. This leads you into Sherwood Forest and along a wide and straight forest ride. After 3/4 of a kilometre a track crosses your path and you go right and along a bridleway that follows the edge of the wood. Eventually you reach the track that you started out on and, after bearing right, you return to the carpark.

The West Leake Hills

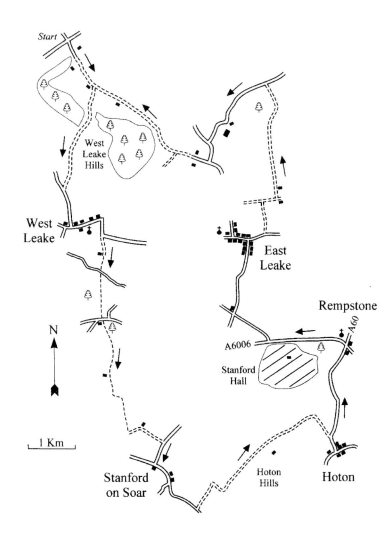

The West Leake Hills

Route Summary
Kegworth Road, West Leake Hills, West Leake, Stanford on Soar, Hoton Hills, Rempstone, East Leake, Crow Wood Hill, Kegworth Road.

Details
Grade — Difficult (v.diff if wet)
Time — 4 hrs
Distance — 29 km: off road — 18 km
                    on road — 11 km
Terrain — Hilly
Surface — fair to good field-edge bridleways, soggy RUPPs
Start Grid Reference — SK 525297
Maps — Nottingham and Loughborough L129.

Introduction
Situated to the south of Nottingham, this hilly area has a number of interesting bridleways and by-ways. Choose your day carefully for this route as, unfortunately, the 4 x 4 fraternity are also keen on using some of the by-ways, and this can make the going very interesting after wet weather.

  The route starts just to the north of the West Leake Hills, within easy distance of the M1 motorway. After crossing the hills, which provide a splendid view of Charnwood Forest further south, the route makes its way though the pretty little village of West Leake, which has an interesting church with an unusual bell tower. After the village there is an almost continuous bridleway section for nearly five kilometres down to Stanford on Soar and then the route traverses the top of the Hoton Hills. It is possible to leave this section out (and the on-road riding that follows) by diverting to East Leake rather than Stanford, but this would miss out the fine views from the top of the Hoton Hills. After a little bit of road riding, the route skirts the edge of East Leake (but skilfully misses most of it) and uses the RUPPs to the east. If the weather has been wet you might want to take your wellies with you! The final return section traverses the top of the West Leake hills and the excellent views to the north-east provide a well earned delight to the end of the route.

Route Description

The route starts at the junction of an old county road and bridleway on the Kegworth Road between Kegworth and Gotham. Park opposite the bridleway and head south-east up a hill called Wood Lane, on a metalled bridleway. After a short distance the lane gives way to a good gravel track with fine views to your left. Just past a new farmhouse there is a track off to the right. Go through the gate and follow a sandy track towards some trees. This is the **West Leake Hills**. The track gives way to a grassy clearing and you enjoy a fun descent down to a farm track. Continue straight on along this for over a kilometre, called Wossock Lane, and eventually it brings you to a road. Go left here down Dark Lane and into the village of **West Leake**.

Follow the road round left, past the church and into the village. The road then goes right and just as it turns left, you continue straight on along a bridleway. Climb the little hill on good track and continue past Manor Farm. Go through a gate and follow the right-hand edge of a field on reasonable track and down to a road. Cross over Brickyard Lane, as it is known, and continue uphill on reasonable track. This section passes through a mixture of arable and grass fields and the going could be difficult in very wet weather. After traversing four fields you come to the Rempstone road. Cross over the road and enter a wood via a small bridle gate. The track through the wood can be very difficult going, but soon you exit the wood by a small bridle gate and continue on along the edge of a couple of arable fields on better track. Just past a barn you will see a footpath sign pointing left. Follow this (it is actually a bridleway) and along a wide grassy track. As you pass into the next field turn sharp left and follow along the edge of this field to a railway line. The bridleway then runs

One of the RUPPS near East Leake

alongside the railway line, becomes a lane, and takes you up to a bridge. Turn left and go over the bridge and head towards Barn Farm. Continue past the farm and down to Leake Lane.

Turn right at the road and go down into **Stanford on Soar**. As the road leaves the village it bears right, but you go left and continue straight on along Stanford Lane. After about a kilometre you will see a bridleway on your left. Follow this up a gravely track, past some woods and onto the **Hoton Hills**. The bridleway is clearly marked with blue waymarkers and although the farming around here is predominantly arable, the field-edge bridleways are well defined. The track does a right turn and then follows around the right-hand edge of the field. Continue along the back of some woods called Rigget's Spinney to a stony track. Follow along the edge of further fields on good track, with fine views of Stanford Hall on your left. Eventually the bridleway becomes a green lane which descends to a rather busy road.

After almost complete off-road so far, we now come to a section which is most definitely on-road. Perhaps a little rest from the mud is welcome, but riding on the main **A60** is not! Turn left onto the road, get your head down and after about 1 1/2 kilometres you come to the traffic lights at the **Rempstone** cross-roads. Turn left for Ashby, past All Saint's Church and continue along the **A6006**. After another kilometre or so, take the first right and then right again for Gotham. This takes you down into **East Leake** to a T-junction where you go right. After c.300 metres you will see a RUPP on your left. This is called Sheeplank Lane and at the time of writing was in an horrendous state. Fisherman's waders would probably be the best attire for navigating this mud that calls itself a lane. Fortunately, the county council have decided that it needed sorting, so the going should be much easier now. Follow the RUPP and eventually you come to a junction of lanes where you go right. The RUPP continues around to the left at a small barn and on up the hill. The track is excellent as you climb the hill, but not so good the other side. A combination of four-wheel drive vehicles and horses (and to that now add bikes!) have served to convert this pretty lane into yet another quagmire, especially after wet weather. Descend as best you can and eventually you come to the road.

Turn left here along Bunny Lane, go under a railway bridge and up to a T-junction. Go left again for East Leake, but before you enter the village, just as the road goes sharp left over a railway bridge, you go right and up a tarmac lane. This goes past the golf course and becomes a bridleway track. Eventually the track bears round to the left for West Leake, but you continue straight on along a field-edge bridleway. The bridleway continues along the edge of the golf course on a good sandy track with interesting views on your right. Follow the track into the woods, through a small bridle gate and out into a field used for grazing. Continue down the left-hand edge of the long field which traverses the top of the West Leake hills with fine views. In the far corner you come to some bridle gates and the track continues on alongside a wood. After passing some barns you arrive back at the track that you started out on. Enjoy a fun descent with superb views on your right back down to the start of the route.

Charnwood Forest

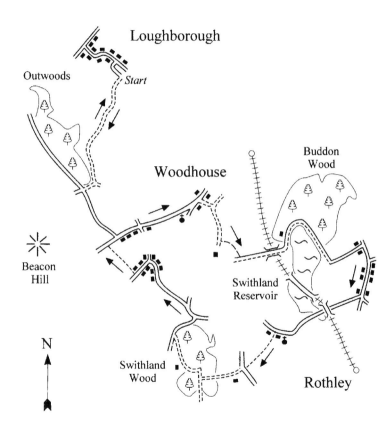

Loughborough

Outwoods

Start

Woodhouse

Buddon
Wood

Beacon
Hill

N

Swithland
Reservoir

Swithland
Wood

Rothley

1 Km

Charnwood Forest

Route Summary
Loughborough, Woodhouse Eaves, Woodhouse, Swithland Reservoir, Swithland, Swithland Wood, The Brand, Woodhouse Eaves, Loughborough.

Details
Grade — Moderate
Time — 2 1/2 hrs
Distance — 24 km: off road — 13 km
                    on road — 11 km
Terrain — Small hills and woodland
Surface — Gravel tracks, open fields and woodland paths
Start Grid Reference — SK 526 176
Maps — Nottingham and Loughborough, L129.

Introduction
The land to the north and west of Leicester rises gently to form a clump of hills called the Charnwood Forest. The highest landmark, Beacon Hill, may be only a little above 900ft, but they are generally regarded with affection by the people of Leicester and have been referred to as 'Little Matlock'. First inspection may give the impression that Charnwood could be an ideal location for off-road biking; however, this is not quite the case. Although there are many footpaths in the area, bridleways do not abound. Until recently, mountain biking was allowed on specified tracks on Beacon Hill. Unfortunately, due to the inconsiderate behaviour of a few, bikes are now banned from this excellent area. It is, however, possible to combine small lanes and bridleways to form a route which provides fun and shows just a little of the beauty of the area.

Although the start of this route may not be very promising, situated as it is on the edge of a housing estate on the outskirts of Loughborough, it actually follows some surprisingly varied countryside. The route uses solid bridleway tracks and small roads and is therefore usually quite easy to ride, even after very wet weather. The route follows bridleways and roads below Beacon Hill to Woodhouse Eaves and Woodhouse and then continues off-road to Swithland Reservoir. A short section on road takes us to Swithland and on good bridleways through the nature reserve of Swithland Wood, to return to the start via Woodhouse Eaves.

Route Description
Park at the carpark at the end of Moat Road, just off Valley road. Follow the track running roughly south by the side of the recreation ground. The stony track, bordered by hedges, opens out and follows alongside a copse to a gate. Continue along, climbing gently below the Outwoods until the track divides. Go left and across the field on a good track towards some houses and the woods. After negotiating a couple of gates, go past the houses, bear right and up to a lane. Turn left here and follow Break Back Lane down to Woodhouse Eaves, where you go left again at the main road and continue on down to **Woodhouse**.

Not long after the left hand bend in Woodhouse there is a lane on the right, Vicary Lane. Follow this track to a T-junction and go right for Rushey Field Manor. Just before the farm, go through a gate on the left and follow the bridleway for Swithland along the bottom of the field. Before the first field boundary, turn right and go up the field to a gate. Follow a grassy track to another gate and onto a lane. Go left here and follow the poorly surfaced lane, over the Great Central Railway and down to the **Swithland Reservoir**.

Follow the lane around the reservoir admiring the attractive scenery, with Beacon Hill in the distance and, if you are lucky, a steam train crossing the viaduct. At the end of the reservoir follow the lane as it does a sharp turn left uphill to the main road. Go right here and down the road to Rothley Plain. At the junction go right for Swithland and Woodhouse Eaves and follow the road down to the other end of the reservoir. Stop here to feed the ducks if you want,

Entering Swithland Wood

and then continue on to Swithland. Just past St Leonards church is a bridleway on your left but, if you are in need of refreshment, the Griffin Inn is but a short distance up the road!

Go through a gate and along the bridleway between houses and then across a field, looking out for Swithland Hall on your left. Go through another small gate and then along a good rocky track to a road. At the road go right, then almost immediately left along a bridleway past a house. This narrow but good track leads into **Swithland Wood** which is a nature reserve and a remnant of the ancient Charnwood Forest. The wood is a favourite with walkers, horse riders and bikers as well as wildlife. The many bridleways are clearly marked with yellow posts, so please keep to them and resist the temptation to go elsewhere. Follow the posts uphill to a T-junction where you go right. After a short distance fork left, then almost immediately fork right and follow the track down and up to a small bridleway cross-roads. Go right here, through a gate and along a good track by the side of a caravan park, eventually to a road.

At the road, go right and down the hill past The Brand, a favourite spot with local rock climbers, to a junction. Here you go left and then left again for Woodhouse Eaves. Stop off at the Wheatsheaf Inn if you are in need of further refreshment and then continue up and down to the cross-roads in Woodhouse Eaves. Turn left here and about 50m past the Curzon Arms is Mill Lane on your right. Go up this steep little hill, called Windmill Hill, which becomes a track and leads into the woods. Take a rest at the top on the bench (you may well need it if you have visited all the pubs *en route*!) and then leave the wood via a small gate. Go down the field to another two gates and a small carpark and on to the road, where you go right. Take the next road left up Break Back Lane and return via the bridleway you started out on to Loughborough.

Hill climb near Monk's Grave Motte, Old Ingarsby (Barkby route)

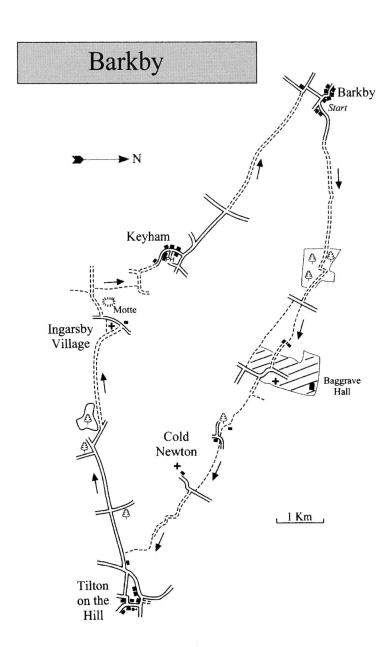

Barkby

N

Barkby
Start

Keyham

Motte

Ingarsby
Village

Baggrave
Hall

Cold
Newton

1 Km

Tilton
on the
Hill

Barkby

Route Summary
Barkby, Barkby Holt, Baggrave Hall, Cold Newton, Tilton on the Hill, Ingarsby Village, Keyham, Barkby Thorpe, Barkby

Details
Grade — Difficult
Time — 4 hrs
Distance — 27 km: off road — 18 km
                    on road — 9 km
Terrain — gently rolling hills
Surface — well-defined sometimes soft bridle ways and good tracks
Start Grid Reference — SK 636 098 (on L140 but only for a very
                    short distance)
Maps — Kettering, Corby & surrounding area L141. (Start GR
      SK 650 098)

Introduction
Situated just six miles north-east of the centre of Leicester, it is hard to believe that such quiet villages can exist so close to the noise and bustle of a city. Time seems to have passed Barkby by, but in fact it is within easy reach of the main trunk routes. The presence of the Hall is highlighted by the parkland between Barkby and Barkby Thorpe.

The route itself starts easily enough along Barkby Holt Lane and continues east along well-defined bridleways past the medieval villages of Baggrave, Lowesby, Cold Newton and almost to Tilton on the Hill. By contrast the return journey is along disused county roads via the medieval villages of Ingarsby and Keyham.

Those wishing to extend the route will note that it crosses the Tilton and Quenby route and it is possible to combine the two. Indeed the whole area is so rich in well-defined bridleways and disused county roads it is often difficult to know when to stop!

Route Description

The route starts at the charming village of **Barkby** on the north-east outskirts of Leicester. It is hard to imagine that such peaceful and pleasant countryside can lie so close to a major city like Leicester. From the centre of the village follow the road east for Beeby and 100 m past Thorpe lane on the right take a lane left. This is Barkby Holt Lane. Follow the lane on tarmac for over 2 km, when the RUPP becomes a good solid track which heads into some woods. The track does a left turn in the woods by a large tree and then arrives at a T-junction. Turn right, along what is called Ridgemere Lane, and enjoy a fun ride on an excellent track. This eventually reaches a small bridle gate, through which you exit the wood and continue along the edge of a couple of fields to arrive at a road.

Up to this point the off-road has been easy, but now we must tackle some arable fields. Go through a gate on the opposite side of the road and cross a couple of fields (carry!) and then along the left-hand side of an hedge to arrive at Waterloo Lodge Farm. Continue through the farm and along the drive, which eventually takes you to a road in **Baggrave Park**. The Hall is down the road to your left, but we continue straight on. After about 250 m the road bears right, but we continue through a bridle gate and then a second one, and into a lane. This half kilometre section of bridleway can be quite fun, particularly if the local hunt have just been through! Shoulder your bike and wade through the mire, eventually to arrive (thankfully!) at a gate.

This is the point at which we join the Tilton and Quenby route. It would be quite feasible to turn left here and join this route if you wanted to extend your travels, but this would be to miss some excellent off-road yet to come. We, therefore, continue straight across the field along the Midshires Way to arrive at a small bridle gate. The fields here are used for grazing and are therefore much easier to ride. Continue across another field and then down a fenced bridle way to the front of Inkerman Lodge. Go through three gates and along a track towards a coppice. Note the old railway carriage (how the hell did that get here?) and wend your way through the wood.

On leaving the wood you find yourself at an excellent little spot for a quick snack, by White's Barn. Cross over the road to a pond and follow the bridle way sign which indicates that you are still on the Midshires Way and that Cold Newton is one mile. This part of the route crosses parkland associated with Lowesby Hall, which can be seen in the distance. The going is excellent, so enjoy a fun descent across two fields used for grazing to arrive at a small bridge over a stream and a gate. Go through this, up and over a little hill and down to another gate and bridge. Turn right along the bottom of the field, through a gate and then uphill to arrive at a road. This is Skeg Hill near the medieval village of **Cold Newton**. A little further up the hill you will see the track for Hamner's Lodge and a sign left indicating the Midshires Way to Tilton Lane 1 1/2 miles. Follow this track downhill, over a stream and steeply up past the farm. The track continues to climb with excellent views to the left. Follow the obvious track which takes you out into a large field. Head straight for the guide post and then go right and up the field. After going through a gate, follow around the left-hand edge of a field towards some barns. Go through another gate, bear left and out onto **Tilton Lane** via a final gate.

After so much off-road you will perhaps be quite relieved to have a little rest! If you diverted to join the Quenby route you will rejoin the Barkby route at this point. Follow the lane west for about 2 1/2 km where you will see the road forks and you go downhill to the right. About 400m on your left you will see a gate and a grassy track heading off across a field. Follow this ancient road to arrive at a gate and then continue straight on along a line of old trees. At the next gate continue on along the top of the field on a grassy track, which still show evidence of the original road, to another gate. Continue following a line of posts down to a gate where you go right and along a track between trees. After going through a couple of gates you arrive at the medieval village of **Ingarsby**, still clearly visible as a mass of bumps and hollows. Turn left and enjoy a humpy bumpy descent, through the remains of the old village, to a bridle gate and onto the road. Turn left and just past the stream you go right at a gate. There are no waymarkers here, but go through the gate and climb uphill on the ancient road . As you climb steeply up on a good track, you will notice the remains of an old fortification on your right. This is called Monk's Grave **Motte** and is worth a quick inspection.

Soon you arrive at a gate and cross the following field to the far corner where there is a further gate which has a red waymarker. Go through this gate and after about 50m you will see a gate into a field on your right. There is no waymarker here, but this is a bridleway. Go through the gate and cross the field to another gate and down the left-hand side of a field past Keyham High Leys Farm. Go through a further gate in the bottom corner, cross over the disused railway via a bridge and on good bridle way down to a farm track. Turn left here and follow the track, but where it bears left, you go right and through a bridle gate. Follow the bridleway which eventually takes you into the village of **Keyham**.

Follow the lane through Keyham (look out for the Dog and Gun on your right) and uphill to a T-junction. Turn left and then take a right fork along Keyham Lane. Soon you come to another T-junction at Scraptoft Lane, but opposite you will see a gate, through which you go. This section of old county road is well defined and marked with yellow waymarkers. The track is good to excellent following alongside the edge of fields and eventually brings you out at the main road at Barkby Thorpe. Carry straight on and then immediately right and back to the start at Barkby.

Carr Bridge "crossroads" (Tilton & Quenby)

Tilton and Quenby

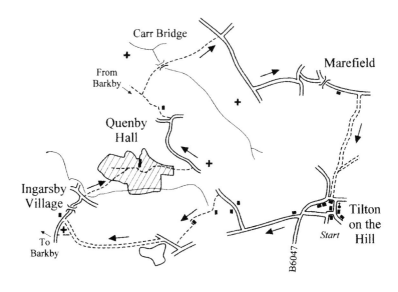

Carr Bridge

Marefield

From
Barkby

Quenby
Hall

Ingarsby
Village

Tilton
on the
Hill

Start

To
Barkby

B6047

N

1 Km

Tilton and Quenby

Route Summary
Tilton on the Hill, Sludge Hall Hill, Old Ingarsby, Quenby Park, Carr Bridge, Marefield, Tilton on the Hill.

Details
Grade — Difficult
Time — 3 hrs
Distance — 24km: off road — 14km
                   on road — 10km
Terrain — Gently rolling hills
Surface — Bridleways across pasture and green lanes
Start Grid Reference — SK 743 057
Maps — Kettering, Corby and surrounding area, L141.

Introduction
The land to the east of Leicester is much quieter and less affected by ravages of modern day agriculture and industry than that to the west. As one goes east, the land starts to rise gently and the houses on the outskirts of the city soon give way to fields, quiet lanes and villages. Here the fields are often small and there is much evidence of old, long deserted villages and tracks. In fact, there are so many tracks in the area it is difficult to decide which to use for the best possible route. This particular route starts at Tilton on the Hill, which has the reputation of being the highest village in the county, all of 700ft above sea level. An alternative title for this route could have been 'An exploration of the deserted villages of Leicestershire', as there are many such in the area. A prime example is Ingarsby, which was originally settled by the Danes in the late 9th century and depopulated in 1469 when the Abbey of Leicester, who owned the manor, decided to enclose the area for sheep and cattle farming. The old hall still remains and there is clear evidence of the village in the neighbouring fields. Other deserted villages *en route* include Baggrave, Lowesby and Cold Newton, the latter being particularly worth a visit.

Route Description

Start at the cross-roads in the centre of Tilton on the Hill and go south, past the church and through the village. Take the first right and then, after going sharp left, take the next right, along Back Road to the B6047. Go left here, then right and along Tilton Lane. You will notice that after about 200m there is a gate on the right which leads into a field. This is in fact a gated road which leads past Hamner's Lodge Farm and on towards Cold Newton village. Although this is almost to good too be missed and is well worth a visit at a later date, our route continues along the road to a cross-roads, where we go right. Enjoy a speedy descent down Sludge Hall Hill, past the farm, and then after about 300 metres you will see a track on the left. Go through the red double gates, where there is a bridleway sign, and along the firm track which then splits, left leading up towards Cold Newton Grange and right leading straight ahead. The bridleway, as shown on the map, goes left and just before the farm, through a gate on the right. According to the map, the bridleway now crosses the arable field to the far right-hand corner, where there is a gate in the right-hand boundary. The occupants of the farm, however, have indicated that most users of the bridleway continue straight on at the division in the track and then along the bottom of the field to this gate. At any rate, go through the gate and follow the edge of the field with the boundary now on the left towards a farm. Go through two sets of large gates, along in front of the farm, and then bear left and up to a small red gate and a solid track. Go right and follow the track along to the road.

At the road go right and after about 300m you will see a gate on the left and a wide grassy track across the field. Follow this ancient road to arrive at a gate and then continue straight on along a line of old trees. At the next gate continue on along the top of the field on a grassy track which still shows evidence of the original road, to another gate. Continue following a line of posts down to a gate where you go right and along a track between trees. After going through a couple of gates you cross the medieval village of **Ingarsby**, still clearly visible as a mass of bumps and hollows. The track leads to Ingarsby Old Hall and the road.

Bridleway from Marefield to Tilton on the Hill

Go right and follow the road round and down to a T-junction. Just opposite is a bridleway sign. Follow the bridleway over a stream and up hill, through a couple of gates, climbing the hill towards **Quenby Hall**. Eventually you arrive at a small red bridle gate which leads onto the main drive. Go right and along the drive towards the rather grand looking hall. Bear right before the main gates and go through a small bridle gate and around the southern perimeter of the hall to regain the track at the back. Follow this track through a couple of gates to arrive at a road. A left turn takes you along a road to a junction at White's Barn.

At the junction go right for Lowesby and just past the trees, on the left, is a bridleway sign. Follow this through the woods to a small gate, into a field and on to another gate. Cross the drive in front of Inkerman Lodge, through a small gate, and then bear right across the field. Go through another gate, bear left, cross a field, through another gate and across to a junction of bridleways. The bridleway ahead leads to Baggrave, another medieval village site, but our route goes right. Follow down the left-hand edge of three fields, at the bottom of the last one of which, you follow the track right and up to a gate. Go through this and bearing slightly right, descend to a very old bridge, **Carr Bridge**, and incongruously, a road signpost! Why this should be here is not clear, except that it marks the inter-section of our bridleway and a footpath from Baggrave to Lowesby, and was obviously an important junction in the past. At any rate, we continue straight up the hill, following the left-hand side of the field on a reasonable track through four gates, to arrive at a road.

Go right and along the B6047 for about 1 km and then turn left for Marefield. Follow the pot-holed road down to a junction where you go left, then right and along gated roads to the hamlet of **Marefield**. About 300m past the buildings along the lane, on the right-hand side, is a bridleway sign. Go through a gate and down a good stony track, fording a couple of streams. Continue on uphill (a nice little hill climb), eventually arriving back at the start of the route in Tilton on the Hill.

Field road to Thorpe Satchville (Burrough Hill)

Burrough Hill

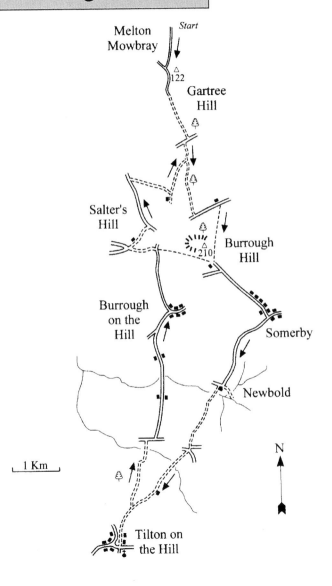

Start

Melton
Mowbray

△
122

Gartree
Hill

Salter's
Hill

Burrough
Hill

△
210

Burrough
on the
Hill

Somerby

Newbold

1 Km

N

Tilton on
the Hill

Burrough Hill

Route Summary
Melton Mowbray, Gartree Hill, Burrough Hill, Somerby, Newbold, Tilton on the Hill, Burrough on the Hill, Salter's Hill, Gartree Hill, Melton Mowbray.

Details
Grade — Very difficult
Time — 4 hrs
Distance — 27 km: off road — 16 km
                    on road — 11 km
Terrain — Rolling hills, farm land and green lanes
Surface — Green lanes, grass and gravel, field bridleways
Start Grid Reference — SK 755 157
Maps — Nottingham and Loughborough L129; Kettering and Corby
       L141

Introduction
The route starts in Melton Mowbray and makes extensive use of the excellent unclassified county roads that extend southwards to Tilton on the Hill. Although there are many bridleways in the area, for example, between Owston and John O'Gaunt, these must be treated with care and are only for the truly committed mud-plodders!

A highlight of the route is Burrough Hill. This is a site of archaeological interest and is managed by Leicestershire County Council. The top of the hill is an Iron Age fort and there is evidence of occupation from the 3rd Century BC to the 4th Century AD. More recently the area within the fort was used for country sports in the 16th and 17th century and also for the Melton Hunt Races. Nowadays, the whole area is protected by law so **no bikes**, except on the bridleways! The hill stands at a magnificent height of 690 ft above sea level and provides a grand view of the surrounding countryside.

Take time to visit the viewpoint and have a picnic, but keep off your bike. Further south, the route makes good use of some excellent un-classified county roads which lead from Newbold to Tilton on the Hill via Red Lodge Road, and back via Marefield Lane.

Route Description

The route begins to the south of Melton Mowbray, just off the B6047, at grid reference SK 755 157. At the end of the road a track continues roughly southwards, this is called Sandy Lane on the maps. The track passes through a few gates and along the left-hand side of some fields, over **Gartree Hill** and eventually down a rutted lane to a road. Turn right and then first left down a green lane. This delightful track (at first!) passes through a couple of gates and down into a dip which can be boggy. Unfortunately, this lane can get difficult in the wet, as it is well used by horses. Struggle on and directly ahead you will see **Burrough Hill**, an impressive little ridge in these parts.

Soon you arrive at a road where you have two possibilities. The first is to go left and towards Home Farm. Just past the farm and on the right is a bridleway which crosses an arable field, leading up towards Burrough Hill. In autumn and winter, when the field has prob-ably been ploughed, this can be almost impossible and should only be attempted by the really determined! After a dry spell in summer, however, it is quite possible. At the top of the field you enter the Dalby Hills Country Park via a small bridle gate. Continue straight on, across a path, and up the hill, following the bridleway, to arrive at a gate. This leads into an open field, the other side of which you cannot see at first, due to the curve of the hill. Have faith and carry straight on across and you will see a smaller gate. Continue on through this and down another field and up to a further gate. After going through this, aim for the main farm buildings straight ahead and the track which goes right for Burrough Hill or left to the carpark.

The second possibility would involve going right at the lane and towards Moscow Farm. Bear left at the farm and after 500 metres

The ford near Newbold

a road comes in from the right. Continue straight on and after another 500 metres or so there is a cross-roads, although it does not immediately look like it at first. This is in fact a very ancient road called Salter's Road. The tracks are signposted 'Unsuitable for Motor Vehicles'. That going right and up Salter's Hill says 'Field road to Thorpe Satchville' (we will meet this on our return journey) and that left 'Field road to Burrough Hill'. Go left and along the left-hand side of the field, through a gate and up past the top of Burrough Hill to the track which leads to the carpark.

From the Burrough Hill carpark continue straight on along road for **Somerby**. As you come into the village the road bears left (to the Stilton Cheese Inn!), but you turn right (a sign advertises the Somerby Riding School) and along a tree-lined road which leads down to **Newbold**. The road bears right and, just after the house, you will see a gravel road on the left. There is a sign saying 'Unsuitable for Motor Vehicles' here, but it was playing dead the last time I saw it! Follow the gravel track down, over a muddy ford and on uphill slightly on a good track to a road. Go right here and then at the junction where the road for Halstead continues straight on, take this but turn immediately right and through a metal gate. Follow the right-hand field boundary to the bottom, through a muddy ford and then a gate. Carry on uphill along a lane, through a gate, over an old railway bridge and up past Red Lodge Farm, from which the lane derives its name. The lane continues on tarmac and eventually arrives at **Tilton on the Hill**.

Stop for refreshments in the village if you like or take time to look at the 12th century church of St Peter, which apparently has some interesting gargoyles, and then return via the lane by which you entered the village. Where the lane divides, go left and down a gravel track, called Marefield Lane, which fords a couple of streams and arrives at the road near Marefield. Turn right and then take the first left along a lane for **Burrough on the Hill**. At Burrough Court turn right, then first left for Great Dalby, and zoom down the hill. At the Salter's Road junction at the bottom of the hill go left where it is signposted 'Field Road to Thorpe Satchville'. Climb the excellent track up **Salter's Hill** to the lane at the top, where you turn immediately right and go along a good track to a gate. Cross a field to another gate and through this to a green lane. The track becomes grassy and bears right after another gate and out onto a road, where you go left. After about 1 km you will see a metal gate on the right. Go through this and follow the obvious track through three gates and downhill to some farm buildings, where you go left and along a tree-lined green lane. The track goes through a gate, beyond which it can be very boggy, but eventually opens out and onto the track that we started out on. Turn left here and return via the track and Gartree Hill to Melton and the start of the route.

Launde Abbey

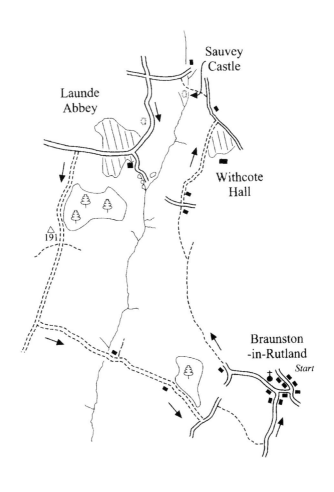

Sauvey Castle

Launde Abbey

Withcote Hall

191

Braunston
-in-Rutland

Start

1 Km

N

Launde Abbey

Route Summary
Braunston-in-Rutland, Withcote Hall, Sauvey Castle, Launde Park, Leigh Lodge, Braunston-in-Rutland.

Details
Grade — Difficult
Time — 2 1/2 hours
Distance — 19 km: off road — 14 km
                    on road — 5 km
Terrain — Gently rolling hills
Surface — Field edges and hard-pack tracks
Start Grid Reference — SK 833 066
Maps — Kettering, Corby & surrounding area L141.

Introduction
The start of this pleasant little route is in Rutland, a county that has never quite accepted being just another district of Leicestershire and has only recently been restored as a county in its own right! The majority of the off-road is on field-edge bridleways, some of which can be a little difficult in wet, but on the whole they are very good. The bridleway which runs along the top of the hill towards Ridlington, for example, is mostly solid track and provides fine views of the surrounding countryside.

Other interesting sights to be seen on the route include Launde Abbey, which nestles in a hollow of hills and is surrounded by parkland and woods. The original priory was founded in 1119, but was dissolved by Henry VIII in 1538. The house is 17th century and is owned by the Diocese of Leicester. Also worth looking out for, although slightly hidden by trees, is Sauvey Castle. Nothing remains of the castle itself, but the motte and bailey construction, which uses the confluence of two streams for a moat, can be clearly seen.

Route Description

Start at the Blue Ball Inn in Braunston-in-Rutland, a charming village with many pretty little cottages. Take the Leighfield and Ridlington road out of the village and where the road goes left you continue straight on along a no through road. The road soon deteriorates and becomes a track and then a bridleway which follows a couple of long fields. This section is probably the most difficult part of the route in wet. At the end of the second field bear left through a gap and into a field with a much used track along the left-hand side. Follow this up to the top left corner, through a gap on the left and into a large ploughed field. Fortunately, the right-hand edge is fenced off and (hopefully) not ploughed. Continue along this with the boundary on the right, through a gap and straight on to the end of the field. Follow the boundary round left past a new gate to a second gate. Go through this and zoom downhill, with a field boundary on the left, to the bottom. Here you will find a gap on your left which leads through to the track from Withcote Lodge. Go right (straight on) and along the track to a house and a lane.

Opposite is a lane with a sign saying 'Bridle Road to Withcote'. Follow this, past the farm with interestingly painted farming equipment in the front garden, to a gate. Continue along a tree-lined track until you arrive at some barns, with a view of the pool and **Withcote Hall** ahead (it can be a bit mucky here!). Turn left just past the barns and follow the edge of the pool round to a pair of large gates. Continue straight on along a stony track across parkland and in front of the house. You arrive at a paddock, go through two gates, and onto a drive. This takes you past a house and stables to arrive at the road.

Turn left at the road and go uphill and then down to the bottom, about 1/2 km. At the bottom is a bridle gate on the left which leads into a field. The way ahead here is not too clear at this point, however, cross diagonally right to a couple of gates. Go through the left-hand gate and follow the field boundary on your right to another gate, which takes you down into a little dell with a stream. Continue straight on through a gate and out into a field where, just to your left

Launde Park

is the site of Sauvey Castle. Bear right and follow along beside the stream to a small gate and then cross the field to another gate and the lane.

Go left at the lane and uphill, taking first left for Launde Abbey. Zoom down the hill and struggle your way up the other side, eventually arriving at **Launde Abbey**. Take time to admire the old building, set in front of parkland, with the monastic fish ponds on the left. Turn right in front of the abbey and sweat your way up hill. At the top of the hill turn left along a track with a bridleway sign. Continue straight along this track, over a cattle grid and along by the side of a wood. After a while the track bears to the left, but you carry straight on, through a gate (no sign) and across a field. Soon you arrive at a gate, cross a short stretch of field in front of the farm to another small gate, and then along the bottom of the field by the side of the wood to yet another gate. The reasonable track now bears left and goes around the edge of the field to a gate in the far corner. After passing through this you arrive at a bridle crossroads. Right leads down to Belton-in-Rutland and left down into the broad valley of the River Chater. We continue straight on along an excellent high-level track (well anyway, it's high for the Midlands!).

Too soon we arrive at a large barn on the left, just past which is a track with a bridleway sign. It is very tempting to continue straight on, eventually arriving at Ridlignton, but charming Rutland village though it is, it does not have a pub! Our route turns left through an impressive entrance and descends a hill to the River Chater and Leigh Lodge. At the bottom we cross over the river, go past the lodge and continue up hill along the drive. The track passes a farm and becomes tarmacked, eventually leading to the road. Go left at the road and down the hill. At the bottom of the hill is a bridleway sign on the right. Follow the track along the edge of the field to a gate. Continue along the tree lined green lane, which becomes a long field, to another gate and then on to the road. Turn left and return to the start of the route in Braunston, and a drink in the pub if it's still open!

Ashby Canal near Gopsall Park (Twycross route)

Twycross

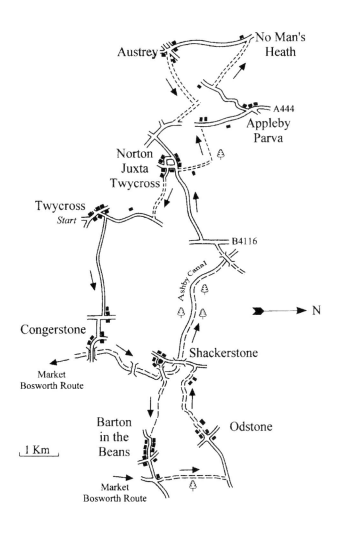

Twycross

Route Summary
Twycross, Congerstone, Ashby Canal, Shackerstone, Barton in the Beans, Odstone, Shackerstone, Ashby Canal, Norton Juxta Twycross, Appleby Magna, No Man's Heath, Austrey, Norton Juxta Twycross, Twycross.

Details
Grade — Difficult
Time — 3 1/2 hrs
Distance — 36 km: off road — 20 km
                    on road — 16 km
Terrain — Gently undulating
Surface — Some difficult field-edge bridleways, but mostly solid tracks
Start Grid Reference — SK 335 050
Maps — Leicester and Coventry L140.

Introduction
The shape of this route may seem a little odd, having two sections at either end that could be left out if required. This, however, would miss out some excellent old county roads which are really fun to ride. The route starts in the village Twycross, famous for its zoo and those tea- drinking chimpanzees seen on the adverts. A short section of the Ashby Canal is used and then the first of the excursions is made. A bridleway takes you into the village of Barton in the Beans, formerly known as Barton Fabis, where in Roman times, believe it or not, beans were grown. Two sections of excellent unclassified county roads bring you back to Shackerstone (and its steam railway), and then onto the Ashby canal again.

This section is perhaps the prettiest stretch of the canal and is very pleasant to ride on a summers evening. After a little bit of road riding and a tricky section of bridleway, we come to the other end of the route and the second 'excursion'. This uses an excellent old road called the Salt Street, apparently used in Roman times for the transport of salt from Cheshire to the south. After a fun little hill climb and a short section of permissive path, we return to the Salt Street and an unclassified county road takes us almost back to Twycross.

Route Description

Start in the village of Twycross and head north along the A444. Take the first right on the B4116 for Snarestone and then right again for Bilstone and Congerstone. Follow the lane which, after a couple of little turns, then runs dead straight towards the village of Bilstone. This is known locally as the 'straight mile' and is a good opportunity to get warmed up. At the village bear right and then immediately left for **Congerstone**. Go over the bridge and then right at the Horse and Jockey pub for Carlton. Follow the road up to the canal bridge and then descend to the canal towpath alongside the Ashby Canal.

At this point it is possible to join the Market Bosworth route (which would need to be done in reverse!) by following the canal south. Our route, however, follows the canal north (go left). Please take care and watch out for people fishing and walking. After a peaceful ride along the canal you arrive at **Shackerstone** and bridge 52. Unfortunately, it is still too early to have a drink at the Rising Sun Pub (unless you must), so leave the canal and go left and over the canal bridge. Take the left fork which goes under the railway bridge. Although there is a sign saying 'Private. Access only', this metalled lane is a bridleway. Follow the lane uphill to some barns and then continue straight on and along the left-hand side of an arable field. Soon you arrive at a bridle gate and, after going through this, you follow the bridleway alongside a little new plantation. Bear left at the end and continue along the bridleway between a hedge and a wire fence. Unfortunately, this can be very difficult after wet, as it is always in the shade. Cross a farm track by a barn (and farmer's junkyard) via two bridle gates. Continue along the fenced-off bridleway on much better ground until you come to the village of **Barton in the Beans**. Continue straight on through the village and up to the cross-roads.

At this point you might like to stop for refreshments at Manor Farm Tea Room, which is just on the corner, on your right — a favourite with cyclists at weekends in the summer. The route continues straight on across the cross-roads and out of the village. As the road bears left you will see a lane on the right. This would be the point at which you would rejoin our route, if you have been keen (and fit!) enough to do the Market Bosworth route as well. On the left you will see Green Lane. Follow this delightful pebbly track along and then downhill to a stream. Ford the stream at high speed if you dare, and then continue up the wooded track. Eventually you arrive at a road, where you go left. This brings you down to the crossroads at **Odstone**. Carry on across, along Hall Lane and just past Ivy House Farm, bear left through some gates, where there is a red waymarker. This old by-way takes you round past Odstone Hall and, after going through into another field, starts to descend. The by-way is usually in good condition, even after wet weather and you should be able to enjoy a fun descent. Eventually the track takes you under a disused railway bridge and up to Tivey's Farm. Go past this and down to a road, where you go left. The road takes you over another disused railway bridge (the entrance to **Shackerstone** Station) and then to a canal bridge. Descend to the canal tow-path via a gate on the right-hand side of the road.

This is the Ashby Canal again and this next section follows what is arguably its most beautiful stretch. The canal skirts along the edge of Gopsall Park and is very wooded and rich in wildlife. On the canal tow-path go right and follow the canal, taking care with people out walking or trying to enjoy quiet fishing. This section is best enjoyed at a leisurely pace, but all too soon you come to bridge 58. Leave the canal here, go left and over the bridge and down to Gopsall Wharf. (The Ashby canal was built primarily for the transport of coal to the south from the North Leicestershire coalfield around Moira and Measham. In fact regular commercial loads carried on into the 1970's and the last load left Gopsall Wharf in 1982. This is an industrial archeological site, so why not sit down and soak up the atmosphere of times gone by, at one of the picnic benches by the canal!) Follow the lane down to the **B4116**, where you go left.

Take the next right where it is signposted 'Norton Juxta and Austrey'. Follow the lane to **Norton Juxta Twycross** and just as it enters the village you will see Cottage Lane on your right. Follow this unclassified county road past Cottage Farm and towards some trees. On reaching the trees you will see signs indicating that the track is now a bridleway only, which suits us just fine. Go left at the trees and into a field, the left-hand side of which you follow. This is perhaps the least convenient section of the route as the field-edge bridleway is ill-defined and can be very difficult going in wet. Soon you arrive at the main **A444**, where you go right. Fortunately, this road tends not to be too busy and after a speedy descent you come to **Appleby Parva**. Just before the village take the first left where it is signed 'Austrey' and climb the hill steadily up a small lane. At the top of the hill, just past the telecommunications pylon, you will see a track crossing the road. This track is part of the ancient Salt Road and has a history that goes a long way back in time. Go right and follow the track, over the M42 (it must be important, they built a special bridge for it!) and down into the village of **No Man's Heath**. Turn left at the bottom of the hill and follow the lane down to Austrey.

In the village of **Austrey**, take first left along Appleby Hill and then immediately right and up Windmill Lane. Continue up the track where it says 'Unsuitable for Vehicles'. This hedge-lined track is a delight and is the nearest thing to an off-road hill climb that you can expect in these parts. At the top, stop and admire the view behind you (including the M42 in the distance!). Continue along until the lane comes to an end and becomes a well-defined track across a field. At this point the old county road turns sharp left and heads back towards the telecom tower again, but we continue straight on along the track. **This section is not a right of way, but a permissive path**

The Salt Street — No Man's Heath

only, and you are here by kind permission of the landowner, Mr Frisby. After less than 300 metres you will see another track crossing. Go right and follow this bridleway, part of the old Salt Street, eventually arriving at the main road.

At the main A444 go straight on (right) and then soon take the first left for Norton Juxta Twycross. On entering the village go right and up Cock Lane. Follow this round to a little junction at Nob Hill (I kid you not!), where you go left and then first right where it is signed 'Wood Lane Works'. The lane takes you out of the village and soon becomes a dirt and grass track. This is usually in reasonable condition, but can have some gloopy bits after prolonged rain. Eventually the track arrives at a road and just opposite Gopsall Wood. Go right and follow the road back to Twycross and the start of the route.

Market Bosworth

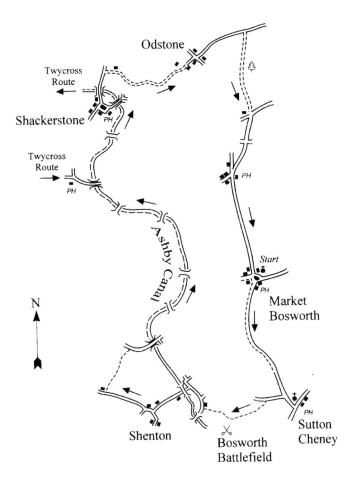

Odstone

Twycross
Route

Shackerstone

PH

Twycross
Route

PH

Ashby Canal

Start

Market
Bosworth

PH

N

Shenton

Bosworth
Battlefield

Sutton
Cheney

PH

1 Km

Market Bosworth and the Ashby Canal

Route Summary
Market Bosworth, Sutton Cheney, Bosworth Field, Shenton, Ashby Canal, Shackerstone, Odstone, Market Bosworth.

Details
Grade — Easy
Time — 2 1/2 hours
Distance — 27km: off road — 15km
                    on road — 12km
Terrain — Farm land and canal tow-paths
Surface — Easy tow-paths, generally good farm tracks
Start Grid Reference — SK 406 030
Maps — Leicester and Coventry L140.

Introduction
This route, situated almost in the centre of England, is possibly the easiest in the book. For that reason it is ideal for those new to off-road riding, for families or those who just want to enjoy a quiet evening ride. The landscape is generally flat, with occasional bumps to make things more interesting. Although there are bridleways in the area, these are often too widely spaced to make a reasonable off-road route. However, by linking together small lanes, gated roads, canal tow-paths and sections of bridleways it is possible to produce an easy but attractive route which is ideal for taking in the sights of an area rich in history, and for a lazy summer's afternoon or evening!

The route is based around the very attractive small town of Market Bosworth and passes through the battlefield site of Bosworth Field. This saw the end of the Plantagenet dynasty of Richard III and the rise of the Tudors in a scurrilous campaign in 1485. The treachery that brought the downfall of the King Richard is still felt today and is marked by a plaque in St James Church, Sutton Cheney, 'Remember before God Richard III King of England and those who fell at Bosworth

Field having kept faith 22 August 1485'. The site is well worth a visit.

The route also makes extensive use of the Ashby canal, a blind tributary of the Coventry canal. This has recently been renovated and the track is now in excellent condition, with seats and even picnic tables at intervals. The canal was actually completed in 1804 and was used to carry coal from the North Leicestershire and Derbyshire coalfields to local markets and then on via the national network of canals to wharfs in Oxford and London. The canal was taken over by the Midland Railway in 1845, but mining subsidence was responsible for the abandonment of the northern length of the canal, and since 1967 the end of the canal has been half a mile north of Snarestone. It must be stressed that bikes do not have a right of way on the canal towpath, but are allowed to use the path upon the purchase of a permit. The address to write to is in the appendix.

Route Description

The route starts in the centre of Market Bosworth and goes due south past the Black Horse Pub and some fine, old half timbered houses. Follow a lane signposted 'Sutton Cheney — Gated Road' to the gate and then down a delightful lane bordering Bosworth Park. Although this is a road, it is more used by cattle than cars, so watch out for the cow-pats! After passing through a second gate carry on up a slight hill to **Sutton Cheney**. This is an interesting little village with a couple of pubs and the old Almshouse tea rooms situated next to the Church of St James. It was in this church that Richard III was said to have prayed before the Battle of Bosworth in 1485 (it did not seem to do him much good!).

If however, you are eager to proceed, then just before Sutton Cheney turn sharp right along Ambion Lane, signposted 'Shenton'. After about 1/2 km you will see on your left Cheney Lane Bosworth Battlefield carpark. Go into this and bear right and down to the bottom where there is a small gate and the start of a bridleway. Follow this on a good track along the edge of fields and through four gates to arrive at the Battlefield visitors centre (another tea stop?). Bear right

Ashby Canal at Far Coton

and go down the drive, as if to leave the visitors centre, and very soon you will see a bridleway on your left. Follow this up and around a small copse to a path and a gate. Although this path is a bridleway (and indeed is used by horses) it is also used by visitors to the battle-field, particularly at weekends. In fact, it might be a good idea to take time out to read the displays which give a graphic description of the Battle of Bosworth Field. In any event, take great care and **go slowly**! Follow the track down and around, through a gate, down the hill, across a farm track and to Shenton Station. This is the end of the Shackerstone steam railway, so take care when crossing the track or you and your bike might get damaged! Go through the carpark and onto the road.

Turn right at the road and continue down past the field on the left where King Richard fell (this is the bit where he cried 'A horse! A horse! My kingdom for a horse') and on up hill slightly to a junction, where you go left for **Shenton**. Pass under the aqueduct and follow the road down to the T-junction. You have a choice here of going left to the Whitemoor Antique Centre for further quick refreshments (can you stand it?) or right if you want to continue on the route. Follow the road round to the left, then right for Sibson. After about 1km you come to Stubble Hills Farm on your right and a bridleway. Follow this, forking right, and continue around the edge of the field on a good track. Go over a stream and past some stables to a single file track through some oak trees. Eventually you reach a road (this last section can be a bit chopped up) where you turn right and continue up to bridge 37 on the Ashby Canal.

Go down onto the tow-path and turn left for Market Bosworth. Follow the path on a good track, but take care where it passes under the bridges as these are quite low and the paths become a little nar-row. This track has been renovated and there are many places to stop and have a rest or picnic, as well as a few pubs being situated not far from the canal. Eventually you reach bridge 52 at **Shackerstone** where you can stop for refreshments at the railway station and admire the trains and so forth or, if you prefer, visit the Rising Sun in the village.

Gated road, Market Bosworth

In any event, continue along the canal tow-path until you reach the next bridge where you finally leave the canal.

Follow the road north over the railway bridge and for about 300m until you see a drive signposted for Tivey's Farm. This is in fact an unclassified county road which eventually leads to Odstone. Go past the farm, bear right, and then down and under a railway bridge. Follow the obvious track and after a while it bears right and then left and starts to climb towards Odstone Hall. The track goes right, around the grounds of the old hall to a bridle gate which leads onto a lane. Follow the lane into the hamlet of **Odstone** and a cross-roads. Continue straight across for Ibstock but after about 1km you will see a track on your right. Follow this wooded green lane (called Green Lane!) down to a ford and climb up on a stony track, eventually reaching a road junction. Cross straight over and return along small lanes via Carlton to Market Bosworth and the start.

Leicester Forest

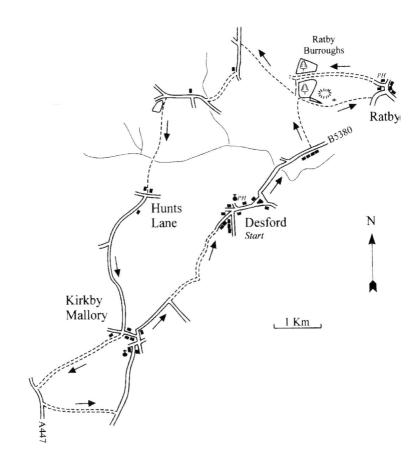

Ratby
Burroughs

PH

Ratby

B5380

Hunts
Lane

PH

Desford
Start

N

Kirkby
Mallory

1 Km

A447

Leicester Forest

Route Summary
Desford, Ratby, Ratby Burroughs, Merry Lees, Kirkby Mallory, Stapleton, Desford.

Details
Grade — Difficult
Time — 2 1/2 hours
Distance — 28 Km: off road — 18 km
                   on road — 10 km
Terrain — Very gently undulating
Surface — Good unclassified roads, but soft woodland bridleways
Start Grid Reference — SK 479 033
Maps — Leicester and Coventry L140.

Introduction
This route is situated on the very outskirts of Leicester. The land to the west of the city is generally flat, arable countryside with a little light industry, and it is perhaps surprising, therefore, that it is possible to produce such a pleasant and enjoyable route. In fact it is quite easy to escape the noise of modern-day life and discover the quiet old tracks that can be found in this area.

The route uses a mixture of small country lanes, unclassified county roads and woodland bridleways. The latter can provide quite a challenge, in the wrong kind of conditions! Bridleways around Ratby are well used by horse riders and can be heavy going in the wet, and bone-jarring after a drought.

The Ratby loop may seem a little contrived, but to leave it out would be to miss the pleasant ride to and from Ratby Burroughs, and the pub in the village!

Route Description

The route starts in the village of Desford, about 8 miles west of the centre of Leicester. From the roundabout in the village go east and take the first left (straight on), the B5380 for Kirby Muxloe. Go down to a T-junction and left following the road down to Newtown Unthank. About 1/2 km after this (opposite some factories - not a pretty bit this!) is a track on the left signed 'Woodland Farm'. This part metalled track is a bridleway and thankfully takes you away from civilisation and into the woods of Ratby Burroughs. The track goes past a house and eventually does a sharp right turn for Woodlands Farm. Continue straight on, however, at a blue waymarker, following the left-hand side of the field and towards the woods. After going through a small gate you descend and arrive at a bridleway junction.

Turn right here and follow along the edge of a field, with the boundary on your left, until you arrive at a large iron gate at the entrance to a wood. Continue straight on into the woods and then follow the edge of the wood, along a path which can be difficult in wet. After a short while the track leaves the wood via a small iron gate and enters a field. Follow along the bottom of the field by the side of a small stream. The track goes through several more bridle gates, all signed with blue waymarkers, until you reach a more definite track. Eventually the track joins the road where you go left for the village of **Ratby**.

In the village go left, then first left past the Bulls Head Pub along the little lane called Burroughs Road. Stop at the Plough Inn if you're in need of refreshments and then continue along metalled road. The road fords a brook and then continues uphill to the woods of **Ratby Burroughs** again. The tarmac ends and becomes a firm track which has now been re-graded as a bridleway. When the track leaves the woods it continues to the ancient moated farm of Old Hays, reputed to have been a home of Lady Jane Grey. Do not continue along this track, but turn left down the edge of the wood along a bridleway, to a small bridle gate and into the wood. The track brings you to a stream and almost in a full small circle (but a very worthwhile one).

Field road from Kirkby Mallory

Go right and over the stream and along a wooded track, which can be extremely soft in places. The track goes through a golf course so keep your helmet on, and after struggling through several soft bits, you eventually arrive at a road.

Turn left at the road and after about 1/2 km, just past a house, go right and down a little wooded track. This delightful little unclassified road is called Coley Lane. At the bottom you pass Coley Cottage and here you have a difficult choice - well actually not that difficult! The lane appears to ford a small river, but to the right is a footbridge. Ford the river if you feel like disappearing up to your armpits in mud or, more prudently, use the footbridge. The lane leads onto a road, where you go right for Merry Lees. Go over the railway bridge and up the hill to the top, where there is a junction. The main road bears right with a road straight ahead. You in fact turn left through a gate with a blue bridleway marker. The bridleway is not obvious, so head straight across the field to the far right-hand corner, go through a bridle gate and along the edge of the field to another gate and a farm track. Cross this, through a gate and across a short stretch of field to a double gate. After going through this and along the field boundary to a further gate you go leftish down the side of a ploughed field to another gate and a large field. Head straight down the field to the bottom and a stream. Squelch your way through the stream and mud, or more sensibly, use the footbridge, and carry on up the track, through a gate and along a lane to the main road (**Hunts Lane**).

At the road go across and down a lane sign-posted 'Brascote and Kirkby Mallory'. After about 3 km you arrive at **Kirkby Mallory** (famous for its race-track which you cannot fail to hear on a Sunday afternoon) and a junction. Go straight across and down Stapleton Lane where it says 'Unsuitable for Motors'. The metalled road passes the race-track (free views of the bike racing!) and just past New Park Farm becomes a good sand and gravel track. Follow this down the hill to a gate by a stream and some woods, a rather tranquil location. Go through a second gate and bear left on a vague track which takes you past a farm to the main road. Go left on the road and after

Ratby Burroughs

approx. 350 metres turn left up a metalled lane (no sign). Just after some houses the tarmac gives way to a good dirt track, but unfortunately this does not last long. Due to the somewhat inexpert use of off-road vehicles the track can be quite rutted. After a tricky descent you reach the road at the bottom, where you go left and return to the other side of the village of **Kirkby Mallory**. In the village go right, then left for Newbold Verdon, and then first right down Desford lane. Follow the lane to a sharp right bend at Fairfields and continue straight on along a track signed 'Unsuitable for Motors'. This excellent track goes over a little ford, eventually becomes metalled, and leads back to Desford and the start of the route.

Rolleston

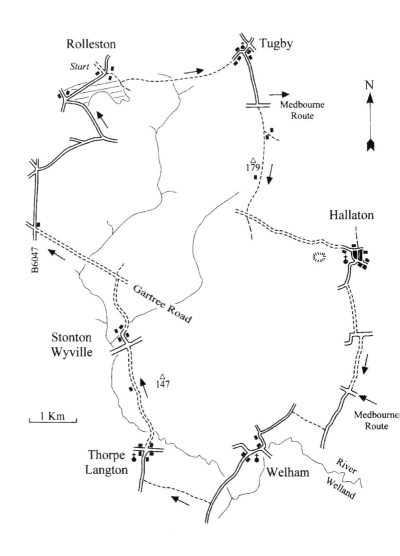

Rolleston

Route Summary
Rolleston, Tugby, Keythorpe Lodge Farm, Goadby Road, Hallaton, Hare Pie Bank, Slawston Hill, Welham, Thorpe Langton, Stonton Wyville, Gartree Road, Rolleston.

Details
Grade — Very difficult
Time — 4 hrs
Distance — 32 km: off road — 19 km
                              on road — 13 km
Terrain — Gently rolling hills and farm land
Surface — Ranging from good solid tracks to field edges
Start Grid Reference — SK 731 004
Maps — Kettering, Corby & surrounding area L141.

Introduction
South of the main A47 road running east of Leicester is an area containing many examples of fine, old unclassified county roads. Two used in this route and worthy of note are Goadby Road which runs from Goadby down into Hallaton, and the Gartree Road. The latter is in fact a Roman Road, now predominantly a minor road or bridleway, which stretches from Leicester, through Medbourne and eventually to Colchester. The section used in this route is little more than a good bridleway track. There are many variations on a theme here. The original route was to have included Noseley Hall and Park, however, the bridleway from Stonton Wyville to Noseley proved so difficult, due to ploughed fields, that it was decided to use the Roman road. Likewise, the bridleway which runs over the hill at Welham looked very tempting. Closer inspection, however, revealed that the bridleway cut across ploughed fields at the top and was therefore very difficult going. Other more hardy souls might like to try these possible alternatives!

A village worthy of note on this route is Hallaton which, together with the neighbouring village of Medbourne, is famous in these parts for the Hallaton Bottle Kicking contest. On the village green, near the conical butter cross, is a plaque which states the following:

This ancient custom is a contest between the villages of Hallaton and Medbourne. Each Easter Monday after a service at the church the hare pie is presented to the rector to divide and distribute. A procession accompanied by a local band then collects the decorated bottles, small wooden barrels, and proceeds from the Fox Inn to the Hare Pie Hill where the pie is thrown to the crowds. This is the starting point of the contest which involves each team trying to get the bottle over the defined boundary. There are few rules and the result is based on the best of three such contests. The beer from the bottles is then drunk by the victors at the Butter Cross.

This route actually uses a very old and quaint lane which runs from Hare Pie Bank down towards Medbourne.

Route Description
The route starts at the signpost at the cross-roads in Rolleston. Follow the track signed 'Bridle road to Tugby', which takes you past the beautiful old church of Rolleston and follows the perimeter wall of the hall. After going through a gate you proceed downhill to a sign. Straight ahead is the bridleway to Goadby, but we go left and through a gate where it is signposted for Tugby. Follow the track down to a gate with a blue marker and continue along the edge of the wood, over a little stream and through another gate, again with a blue waymarker. Thus far, the track has been quite good, but unfortunately at this point it crosses two arable fields. Struggle as best you can (this is probably the most awkward part of the route) and soon you arrive at a stream. Go over a little foot bridge, or if you are feeling a little more adventurous, ford the stream, and bear right following the grass track to a gate. Go through this and follow a good track straight on along

the top of the fields, through two gates and then uphill towards the farm. Before you reach the farm you will see another bridleway on the right from Goadby, but we continue straight on. Just before the farm buildings, we bear right, through a gate, and along a track which leads to a lane, and from there into the village of **Tugby**.

Go into the centre of the village, passing the Black Horse Inn and village stores, to a junction where we go right. Follow the road round, past another pub, and out of the village. The road descends a gentle hill to a junction. At this point it is possible to combine this route with the **Medbourne Route** by going left, if you are feeling particularly energetic! Our route continues straight on, where it is signed 'Field road to Keythorpe'. Go past Keythorpe Hall Farm and along a gravel track, up the hill eventually to arrive at Keythorpe Lodge Farm. Continue past the farm and straight ahead along a good track, passing through a couple of gates. Eventually you arrive at a junction of tracks, which is in fact the Goadby Road. Go left here and follow the track, which after a while becomes metalled, down the hill with good views ahead. Eventually the track crosses a ford and rises up to the village of **Hallaton**. Look out for Castle Hill, a superb example of a motte and bailey castle, on your right as you enter the village. It is thought that this was probably built in the 12th century to protect the surrounding iron workings. As you approach the village, go past some farm buildings and then turn right, down a poor road, which leads into the centre of Hallaton.

Hallaton is a very quaint and interesting little village and it is well worth visiting the village green, where you will see the Butter Cross and the plaque commemorating the Hallaton Bottle Kicking contest. After refreshments at the Bewicke Arms, take the road out of Hallaton towards Cranoe. As the road climbs out of the village and bears right, you continue straight on (left) and along a hedged track and down to a gate. Follow the field boundary on your left through a couple more gates, along an ill-defined track, to arrive at a road. Go left and after 100m turn right and up a dirt lane. Follow this up past Slawston Hill to arrive at a cross-roads. If you were brave enough to include the **Medbourne Route**, this is the point at which you rejoin.

Continue straight across the road and down Green Lane and after about 1 Km you will see a bridleway crossing the road. Go right and through a gate, towards a derelict railway bridge. Follow the blue way-marker and continue on along the left-hand side of a couple of fields on a reasonable track (a bit chopped up by horses) to arrive at another road. Go left here and follow the road into the village of **Welham**, past the Old Red Lion pub. At the junction carry straight on for The Langtons and Kibworth. As the road bears round to the right you will note a road leading straight on and this presents a choice. One option is to follow the Langton road round to the right and then take the bridleway across the top of the hill to Stonton Wyville. This provides a good hill climb and a fun descent, but unfortunately the section across the top is ill-defined and across arable (horrible!) fields. An easier alternative and one that provides a good view of the hills and more pleasant riding is as follows. Continue straight on where the road says 'Unsuitable for Motor Vehicles' and along Bowden Lane. After about 1 Km or so you will see on the right, in some trees, a bridleway sign. Follow the hedged track, which soon opens out and continues along the left-hand edge of a large field on a reasonable track. After going through a couple more fields you arrive at a road. Go right here and up to **Thorpe Langton**.

At the village turn left and pass the Bakers Arms Pub (if you can bear to!) and then first right down a lane signposted 'Unsuitable for Motors'. The track comes down to a ford, which you cross, and go left and through a gate. Follow the right-hand side of the field up to and along the top, soon to arrive at a gate on your right. Go through this and along the left-hand side of the field on a good track, past some barns, eventually arriving at the cross-roads at **Stonton Wyville**. Cross over the road for the village.

In the village turn right where it is signed 'Unsuitable for Motors', opposite the pretty little church. Follow the lane round past some barns and continue on a good track, to arrive eventually at a rather unusual junction of tracks. Here you will find an old sign which informs you that to your right is Glooston 1 mile, whilst to your left is Calton Curlieu (Manor House) 3 miles and Leicester 11 3/4 miles. This is the old Roman **Gartree Road**. Straight ahead is a bridleway which is supposed to lead to Noseley and which looks deceptively easy to start with, but is in fact of very dubious quality further on - not to be recommended except for the terminally masochistic! Our route goes left, following the rutted track through a couple of gates and down to a stream with a muddy ford and, fortunately, a footbridge. It is at this point that you perhaps begin to have a little sympathy for the drivers of the four by four vehicles that attempt this route - but perhaps not a lot of sympathy. Continue uphill on the obvious track through a couple more gates until you arrive at the **B6047**. Go right at the road and after a little over 1 km, right again at Three Gates for Noseley. Take the second left along a gated road to Rolleston and finally right and down the tree-lined drive, to arrive back at the start, in the village.

Blaston Chapel (Medbourne route)

Medbourne

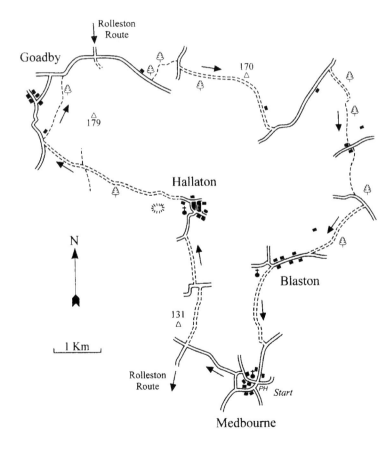

Medbourne

Route Summary
Medbourne, Slawston Hill, Hallaton, Goadby Road, Goadby, Crackbottle Spinney, Fearn Farm, Allexton Wood, Knob Hill, Blaston, Medbourne.

Details
Grade — Difficult
Time — 3 1/2 Hrs
Distance — 28 km: off road — 19 km
                        on road — 9 km
Terrain — A bit hilly
Surface — Excellent gravel tracks and horrible arable bridleways!
Start Grid Reference — SP 800 930
Maps — Kettering, Corby & surrounding area L141.

Introduction
The Roman Gartree Road, used in the previous route, passes close by the village of Medbourne. It is perhaps not surprising then that there was a settlement here in Roman times and evidence of a Roman villa has been found to the south of Medbourne. During excavations in 1877 an elaborate mosaic was found. There is evidence that the settlement continued to be used during the Anglo-Saxon period also — look out for the medieval packhorse bridge by the ancient ford over Medbourne Brook at the start of the route.

      The route uses many excellent unclassified county roads, but take care as some are not obvious on the ground. This is particularly true of the tracks from Allexton, around Knob Hill, and up to Bolt Wood. It is hard to imagine these are actually roads, as there is nothing to be seen on the ground. Fortunately, they mostly cross land used for grazing, so the going is quite good. All other tracks are good, except for the bridleway past Goadby, which is perhaps for the dedicated only!

Route Description

The route starts in the picturesque village of Medbourne. From the centre of the village by the church take the road signed for Hallaton and Slawston and go over the ford by the old packhorse bridge. Follow the road out of the village and take first left, then right for Slawston. The quiet country road makes its way towards Slawston Hill and after going over the disused railway line you will see a sign indicating that the lane on the right is a field road for Hallaton. This charming little wooded lane rises and then descends by Slawston Hill (**131m**) to arrive at a road.

At the road go left, then immediately right where there is a large gate. This is a road, even if it does not look like one! Follow along the right-hand edge of the fields used for grazing and, after going through a couple more large gates, you enter a lane which takes you up Hare Pie Bank, to arrive at a road. Go right here and down into the village of **Hallaton**. Just past the church go left and up Church Gate, past the pretty cottages, and bear right and up a gravel lane to arrive at a junction with a lane which is the Goadby Road.

Go left and follow the road away from the village and as it bears left and descends, note the motte and bailey on Castle Hill opposite. The lane drops down to a ford and then starts to climb steadily. Eventually the tarmac gives way to gravel and the views open out around you. At the top of the hill you come to a junction with the Midshires Way (and the Leicestershire Bike Round). Right will take you down past Keythorpe Farm to the Crackbottle Road, but we continue straight on along the Goadby Road. Follow the track downhill and then up to a lane, where you go right. Almost immediately you will see a bridleway on your right. This next section follows the bridleway across arable fields and can be difficult in wet. An alternative might be to follow the road down into **Goadby** and go right for Tugby. If, however, you decide to tackle the bridleway, follow the lane past Pine Tree Stud, through a gate and across the paddock, bearing left slightly. After going through a small bridle gate you continue on across a large arable field and down to a copse. Continue on a good track

UCR near Allexton Wood

alongside the woods to arrive at a gate onto a road.

Go right (straight on) at the road, past the junction for Tugby and the Midshires Way and, just past Crackbottle Lodge and a spinney, you will see a bridleway sign on your left. Follow this steeply up the side of the woods on a good track. Bear right and follow the edge of the field round with a beautiful view of the hills to the south. Eventually the track takes you down to a lane.

Go right at the lane and after c.100 metres you will see a track on your left and a sign indicating that it is a 'Field Road Horninghold' and that it is unsuitable for motors. Great! Follow this superb gravel track with excellent views as it traverses along a ridge. The track does a turn to the right and down to a farm but you continue straight on along the crest of the hill. The track is not quite so good, but still easy going. Continue through a gate and along the top edge of a field used for grazing. Just after the old trig point (**170m**) the track bears right and down to a gate. Go past Fearn Farm (where they may occasionally do teas) and down the lane to the road.

At the road go left, but note that the old county road to Horninghold continues straight on and through a gate. Follow the road uphill and through woods. After almost 2km, just where the road starts to descend and bear left, you will see a track on your right. Follow this gravel track past some farm buildings, when it becomes a wooded lane, soon to arrive at a gate. After going through the gate, go right and along the top of an arable field, and then bear left and across and down to the far corner, to the right of some woods. Go though the gate and along the left-hand edge of a field to arrive at another gate with a red way-marker. Continue on and through two more gates along the bottom right-hand edge of fields, and then bear to the left of the farm. After a couple more gates you arrive at the road, and opposite another farm.

Cross straight over the road, go through a gate (make sure you close it!), across the farm yard, and follow the vague track uphill, bearing slightly right. At the far end you will see a gate and after this you follow along the top right-hand edge of a field, with fine views to the left. Eventually you arrive at a gate and onto a road.

Go left at the road (straight on) and after a couple of hundred metres you will see a bridleway on your right. Follow the good track along the edge of a couple of fields, towards some woods. Bear right at the woods and follow the bridleway along the back. The excellent track descends the hill and then spoils it all by bearing right and cutting across the arable field. It is interesting to note however, that the track does continue down and around the bottom to rejoin the bridleway again. This is not a right of way, however, and therefore not part of the route. Follow the bridleway around the bottom of another field to join a track and then down to the road.

At the road go right (straight on) and continue into the village of **Blaston**. This quaint village has some fine examples of the yellow-stone houses that are so common in this area. Note the strange clock tower. Follow the road through the village and, where it bears right, you go left where it says 'Field Road Medbourne'. Go past the interesting little church and follow the excellent field road, which descends gently to arrive at the B664. Go right, down into the village of Medbourne and back to the start of the route.

Foxton Locks

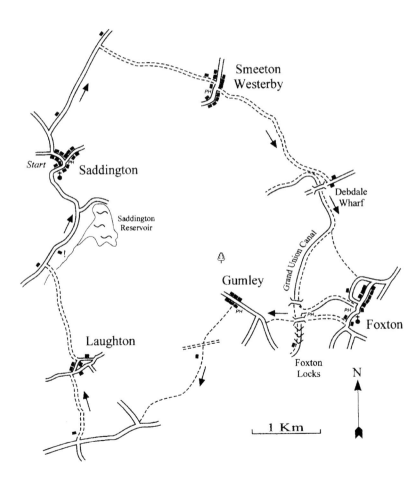

Foxton Locks

Route Summary
Saddington, Smeeton Westerby, Debdale Wharf, Foxton Locks, Gumley, Laughton, Saddington.

Details
Grade — Moderate
Time — 2 1/2 hrs
Distance — 18 km: off road — 12 km
                    on road — 6 km
Terrain — A little bit hilly on occasions
Surface — Excellent stony tracks, some difficult bridleways across fields
Start Grid Reference — SP 658 918
Maps — Kettering, Corby & surrounding area L141.

Introduction
This route uses a number of the superb unclassified county roads in the area around Foxton. Foxton Locks itself is a fascinating example of canal engineering. Started in the late 18th century, the purpose of the locks was to enable barges on the Trent and Soar to link into the canal network to the south and so to reach London. In order to do this they had to surmount a 75ft slope and this was done by creating two five-lock staircases. Finances were a problem so the locks are only wide enough for a single barge, although there is a passing pond half way. Completed in 1812, they must have been a bottle-neck for passing trade. As a consequence a barge lift was created, but the development of the railways made the whole system uneconomical.

Today the locks are a great attraction and Sunday afternoons have a bit of a Blackpool feel about them and are best avoided. Cycling is allowed along this stretch of the Grand Union canal, but not at Foxton Locks. As has already been mentioned elsewhere, in order to ride your bike along the canal tow-path you will need to obtain a cycle permit from British Waterways. The route uses bridleways and unclassified county roads from Saddington to the Grand Union Canal and more excellent UCRs from the Laughton Hills back towards Saddington. The only tricky bit is the bridleway from Gumley to the Laughton Hills and this could be by-passed using country lanes or even the Grand Union Canal itself if the going is soft.

Route Description

Start at the little village of Saddington and go north out of the village. Take the first right for Kibworth and climb up a gentle hill. Near the top you will see bridleways to your left and right. Go right and enjoy a pleasant ride along a charming little wooded lane. The dirt track eventually becomes gravel and leads down into the village of **Smeeton Westerby** (how do they think up these names?). At the road in the village, turn right and then left down Debdale Lane. This unclassified county road is usually in excellent condition. The gravel surface makes for easy riding, even after the worst weather, and crosses mixed farming land. Although this section is flat, the horizon is ringed with low-lying hills which make an interesting backdrop. Continue on this excellent track through a couple of gates and then on up a gentle hill. After going through another gate, the old road follows alongside the Grand Union Canal to a lane. Go right and up to a canal bridge, where you go down onto the canal tow-path; this is **Debdale Wharf**.

     The next section follows the Grand Union Canal for a short distance. This is a beautiful stretch of canal and could be continued to Foxton Locks, but you will need to dismount when you reach the locks and it can be rather awkward when you get there. A better alternative is to take the bridleway which runs parallel with the canal. This actually starts at Debdale Wharf, but finding the start can be difficult. An easier alternative is to take one of the cut-throughs from the canal to the bridleway which runs through the trees. Eventually it arrives at a gate and you continue down the right-hand side of a large field. Follow this around to the left at the bottom and onto a more definite track which leads to a lane. Go right here and follow the lane

Debdale Wharf on the Grand Union Canal

round and into **Foxton** Village. At the junction go right, over the canal bridge and up through the village. At the top there is a track, which is a bridleway, to Foxton Locks. Soon this brings you to the locks, which provide quite an amazing experience in more ways than one. On Sunday the area teems with masses of people and looks like a miniature Matlock Bath or Blackpool. There is a pub (Bridge 61 - Free House), tea-rooms, ice creams, the works, and for this reason the area is best avoided on Sunday afternoons! The Grand Union Canal passes under a bridge and up an amazing set of locks, ten in all. The bridleway continues across the bridge to a gate, down a little lane to a further gate, which takes you into a field.

Continue across the field, which is used for grazing, heading slightly uphill. Follow the faint path, which eventually brings you to a gate and out onto a road. Turn right here and climb uphill to the village of **Gumley**. Go past The Bell Pub and turn left where there is a bridleway sign. Follow this narrow back lane up to a gate and out onto a field. Continue along the top of the field, through some double gates and into another field. In front of you is a large tree. Aim to the left of this and down a steep, fun hill to another gate. After going through this, continue along the right-hand edge of the field, through a couple of gates and across a farm track. Carry on through a couple more gates, past Gumley Lodge, and along a well-defined bridleway which can be difficult going in wet. The track climbs uphill, across an arable field, through a couple of gates, to arrive at a large field used for grazing. The going gets a little easier here, so continue straight on along the top of the hill, bearing left through a gate to arrive at a double gate onto a lane. Take a rest here and admire the view to the east and then go left to a road and T-junction, where you go right.

Follow the road and after less than a kilometre you come to a cross-roads. Turn right where it is signposted 'Gated Road Laughton' and go past Laughton Lodge Farm. Follow the excellent green lane down to a gate and then on uphill to the village of **Laughton**. In the village go right and then bear left for 'Gated Road Gumley and Kibworth'. Where the road bears right you will see on the left an avenue of trees and it is signposted 'Unsuitable for Motors'. The tarmac soon gives way to an excellent stony track and a high speed descent, a rare thing in these parts, so enjoy it! Soon you come to a halt at a gate, through which you continue across a field and slightly to your left. There is no sign of the old road at this point, which seems rather strange. However, after going through gate and across another field, you arrive at a stream and the re-emergence of the old road. Climb up the steep little hill on a firm track to arrive at a road. Turn right here and head back along the road to Saddington, but don't forget to stop off at Jacqui's Tea Rooms (on your right, just before descending the hill) for some well-deserved refreshments.

Fineshade

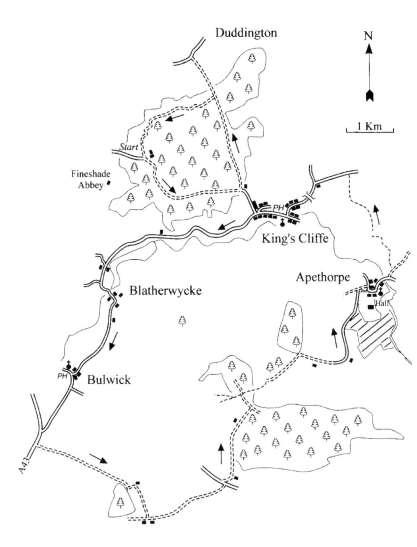

Fineshade and King's Cliffe

Route Summary
Fineshade Forest, King's Cliffe, Blatherwycke, Bulwick, Deene Hall, Apethorpe, King's Cliffe, Fineshade Forest.

Details
Grade — Difficult
Time — 4 hours
Distance — 32 km: off road — 20 km
                    on road — 12 km
Terrain — gently undulating, small hills
Surface — forestry tracks, good grassy bridleways, but also bridleways across arable fields
Start Grid Reference — SP 979 983
Maps — Kettering, Corby & surrounding area L141.

Introduction
This route starts at Fineshade Forest which is managed by Forest Enterprise. A collection of woodlands, it contains quite a diverse variety of flora and fauna. Look out for fallow deer and, if you are lucky, apparently you might even hear the distinctive bark of a Muntjac Deer. Also of interest to those keen on nature, is the Wild Service Tree, which is native to these woods. Its leaves look like those of the maple and the name comes from the Latin *cerevisia*, which means beer. The brown berries were used in the past to sweeten the drink, which was no doubt enjoyed by the occupants of the nearby Fineshade Abbey.

After an easy ride through the woods you come down to the village of King's Cliffe. This interesting little village, still sometimes referred to as the Wooden Spoon village, was once well known for its wooden ware. Indeed, I believe, there is still a wood turner working in the village. King's Cliffe was popular with cyclists in the 1930s, when there was a Youth Hostel located in the village. After some easy riding on road through the picturesque villages of Blatherwycke and

Bulwick, the real work begins. The route follows excellent bridleways all the way to Apethorpe. Try not to upset the locals here as, just opposite the church, you will see the original stocks and whipping post! The next section is probably the hardest part of the route, following a bridleway which occasionally crosses arable fields. Eventually, however, we return to King's Cliffe and finish off with a pleasant ride back through the woods.

Route Description

Park at Top Lodge carpark in Fineshade Forest and follow the road in front of forestry offices, where it says 'horses only'. After 30m or so the road bears left, but you continue straight on along the Jurassic Way. Follow the excellent forestry track through the forest and eventually, where the forest road goes left, you continue straight on, following the bridleway markers. The track goes through a wood yard and down a lane into **King's Cliffe**.

Turn right and follow the road out of the village. Although this next section is on-road, at least it is quiet and takes you through some pretty yellow stone villages. Look out for the old stone cross on your left just after you leave King's Cliffe. Continue along the road with fine views of the lakes to the left, and down into the village of **Blatherwycke**, with its pretty old bridge over the lake. Follow the road along for **Bulwick**, where you turn left. Eventually this brings you down to the main **A43** at Deene Park. Take care here as the road can be busy. Turn left onto the main road, but then after c.350 metres left again, where there is a bridleway sign (there is an earlier bridleway shown on the 1:50 000 OS map, but it is not apparent on the ground).

Climb up the hill on good track, thankfully leaving the main road behind. Continue on good grassy track with a bridleway sign, cross a ditch via a little bridge and after a couple of fields you come to Burn Coppice. . Follow the bridleway round and left to arrive at Forest Lodge, and then on to a junction of tracks in front of some barns. Go left here and enjoy a fun descent. Although there are arable

Blatherwycke Lake

fields on either side, the track is well defined and descends a shallow valley. Eventually, after the track bears left, you arrive at a road.

Cross over the road and climb the farm track towards and past Crossway Hand Farm. Continue along a good farm track, past some barns and down the right-hand edge of the field to a gate. Go through this to a forestry track, where you go left. Follow this to reach a junction of estate tracks, where you go right, through a new plantation, across a wooden bridge and up to a new bridle gate. Continue around the left-hand edge of the field on a less well-defined track and up to a good track alongside some woods. The excellent track cuts across the field to arrive at the corner of Tomlin Wood and then on past Lodge Farm. This estate road eventually reaches a junction where you go right and down a gravel track to the picturesque village of **Apethorpe**. Turn right (stop at the Kings Head for suitable refreshments?) and continue round and past the church.

Leave the village via a small bridge and then take first left, where you see a bridleway sign. Continue along a well-defined track through the trees until you see a bridleway sign on the left. Follow this out of the trees, across the field to a bridge, and head for a gap in the fence. Climb uphill across the arable field (this track is well defined but not to be attempted after prolonged rain) to the top. Turn left here and follow along the top of the field to find an old railway bridge. Go under the disused railway line, turn right and continue around the field on a stony bridleway up and past a copse. At the top of the field go through a gap in the fence and continue along the edge of the field. Continue round and up the left-hand edge of the field to a small bridle gate, which leads into a field used for grazing and with the remains of some WW2 buildings. Carry on as best you can and soon arrive at another bridle gate and onto a road. The hard bit is over!

Descend the hill to a junction and go left for King's Cliffe. In the village turn right by the Cross Keys pub and go along West Street. At the end of the village you come to a junction and you take first right and up the lane that you started out on, back into Fineshade woods. Turn right just before the gate into Fineshade and follow the bridleway for **Duddington**. This takes you along a wide grassy ride which can be very soft in places, but eventually takes you to a forestry track. Continue straight on along this until, as it bears left, you carry on into the woods where it is signed as a bridleway. Soon you cross over another forestry track and the going gets easier. After a few hundred metres you will see a track on your left which doubles back. Go along this and return to the start via an excellent forestry track.

Lyveden New Bield

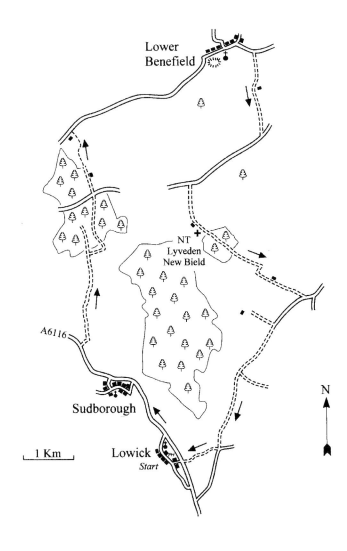

Lyveden New Bield

Route Summary
Lowick, Fermyn Hall, Lower Benefield, Lyveden New Bield , Wadenhoe, Lowick.

Details
Grade — Moderate (could be difficult in wet)
Time — 3 hrs
Distance — 24 km: off road — 14 km
                              on road — 10 km
Terrain — Gently undulating
Surface — Field Bridleways and By-ways, can be soft when wet
Start Grid Reference — SP 978 807
Maps — Kettering, Corby & surrounding area L141.

Introduction
This route starts in the pretty village of Lowick, but the main attraction *en route* is the National Trust property, Lyveden New Bield. This is a shell of an uncompleted lodge begun in 1595 by Sir Thomas Tresham. The lodge is in the form of a cross and has exterior friezes inscribed with religious quotations. Unfortunately, Sir Thomas died before it was completed, and his son, Francis Tresham, was imprisoned in connection with the Gunpowder Plot.

       The building makes an impressive sight on top of the hill, but perhaps more importantly, you can buy an ice cream at the adjacent Custodian's house! The bridleway north of Sudborough is well defined, but the going can be difficult when it enters Fermyn Woods. A quiet section of road riding to Lower Benefield is followed by an excellent by-way. After the ice cream at Lyveden, the bridleway can be a little difficult through Lilford Woods and across arable fields, but soon the going gets easier. The return is made on a fun by-way which takes you all the way from Wadenhoe back to Lowick.

Route Description

Start in Lowick and go north, through the village, and out onto the main A6116. This is the only major bit of main road on the route. About 1km past the village of Sudborough you will see a bridleway sign on your right. Take this dirt track up a little hill and follow on a good track. Eventually you reach a clump of trees where you bear left and continue on towards the woods. When you arrive at the woods you will see a bridleway sign into the woods. You, however, turn right and follow along the edge of the field. Soon you will see another bridleway sign pointing into the woods. Take this and follow the forestry track, where the going can be difficult after rain, eventually to reach a road.

Cross over the road to a solid track, where there is a sign informing you that you are about to risk life and limb by traversing the end of Lyveden Airfield! This is a legal bridleway, but watch out for low-flying gliders and keep your head down. Follow the track and where it bears right, you continue straight on and across a small bridge. The bridleway continues on around the left-hand edge of the arable field and should present no problems in reasonable weather. Exit this field by a small bridle gate and then on along the left-hand edge of the next field to arrive at a lane. Turn right here and follow the quiet road to **Lower Benefield**. At the village you continue straight on, where you join the A427 (only for a very short while!). Bear right out of the village and climb a hill until, near the top, you will see on the right an unsignposted lane. Enjoy a speedy descent until, just past a house, the lane becomes a track. This is a by-way and provides an excellent ride down to a road.

Go right at the road, and after a little under 2 km you will see a track on your left, signed Lyveden New Bield National Trust. The gravel track is a bridleway and climbs uphill steadily. Stop off at **Lyveden New Bield** for an ice-cream and to admire the ruined house in such fine surroundings. Continue on past the house and round to the right, to a bridleway sign which points across a field towards some woods. Cross the arable field on a reasonable bridleway to arrive at

Byway from Lower Benefield

Lilford Wood. The bridleway continues on through the wood on what can be a rather gooey track, but eventually arrives at a gate. Carry on across a field to a bridge and another gate and on up the hill to a gravel farm track. Go right (straight on) and follow the track, but where it turns right, you carry on through a gate and into a wood. This delightful track runs parallel to the farm track and eventually joins it again. Carry on past Wadenhoe Lodge on excellent track with fine views in front and to your right.

When you reach the lane turn right. After less than 1km the lane bears right and towards a farm, but you continue on along a well-defined by-way. This can be wet in places, but on the whole is usually quite pleasant. Follow the track straight on until you arrive at a road. Turn immediate right and up a disused lane. Eventually this brings you down to the main A6116, which you cross with care, to arrive back at the start in the village of Lowick. Time for a pint?

Cottesbrooke

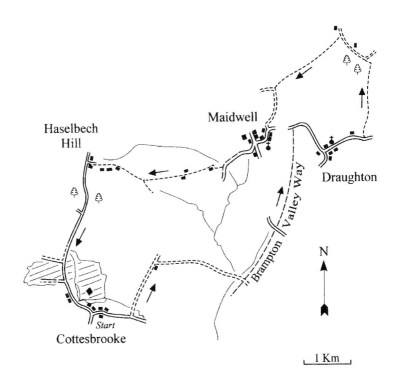

Haselbech
Hill

Maidwell

Draughton

Brampton Valley Way

N

Start

Cottesbrooke

1 Km

Cottesbrooke

Route Summary
Cottesbrooke Park, Brampton Valley Way (Hanging Houghton), Lamport Crossing, Draughton carpark, Draughton, Blue Covert, Maidwell, Haselbech Hill, Cottesbrooke Park.

Details
Grade — Moderate
Time — 2 1/2 hrs
Distance — 25 Km: off road — 17 Km
on road — 8 Km
Terrain — Very gently undulating
Surface — Good gravel tracks, some grassy bridleways
Start Grid Reference — SP 720733
Maps — Kettering, Corby & surrounding area L141.

Introduction
This pleasant route is situated in historically interesting countryside to the north of Northampton, not far from the battlefield site of Naseby. The site marks the important confrontation between the Royalist and Roundhead forces of the Civil War in 1645 and, although not actually included in the route, the museum and monument are well worth a visit.

Although the land is predominantly flat in these parts, there are small hills and ridges that provide good views of the surrounding countryside. The route uses old unclassified county roads and bridleways to the east of Naseby, and also sections of the Brampton Valley Way. The latter is a disused railway line purchased by the County Council in 1987 and developed as a route for walkers, cyclists and horse riders. Many cyclists use this easy linear track, but perhaps few have ventured to explore the possibilities beyond.

Two country houses that are worthy of note are Lamport House and Cottesbrooke. The route is based around the latter and, although the house is not open to the public, there are fine views of it and the surrounding park on the return journey.

Route Description

Leave the charming village of Cottesbrooke and follow the Brixworth gated road east. After about 1km you will see, on your left, some barns and a track with a sign saying 'Unsuitable for Motors' and a by-way sign. Follow this past the barns on a part-metalled track, through a couple of gates and into a wood. Just past a derelict house the track forks and we go right. Follow the long and well-defined track down and across fields, eventually arriving at a little bridge, just past which is the disused railway line, now the **Brampton Valley Way**. Go left and along this, shortly arriving at Lamport Crossing. Cross over the main road (take care!) and continue straight on, eventually arriving at Draughton carpark.

At the lane go right and uphill, soon to arrive at the village of **Draughton**. Bear left into the village and continue straight on past the church. About 1 km outside the village you will see on the left-hand side a track, with metal posts, and a sign saying 'Bridleway to Harrington'. Follow this concrete track past some derelict buildings and along an old World War II airstrip. Near the end of the runway there is a copse on the left, through which passes a narrow path which very soon leads to a solid track. Go left, along this and by the side of Blue Covert. The track leads up to the new A1-M1 link road, just before which you go left, down an obvious track and along the right-hand side of a field. The track enters another field and becomes less defined, but soon arrives at some trees and the Brampton Valley way again. Cross over this and continue straight on along a rutted but ride-able track. At the far end of the large field the track divides and we go left, down the right-hand side of the field. Soon we reach a gate, through which the track continues across grazing land to arrive at another gate and onto a lane on the outskirts of **Maidwell**.

Go right and follow the road through the village to the main road. Note the interesting gate, by the side of which is a stone with an

Bridleway near Maidwell. Repair time.

inscription informing us that the gateway was restored by a Reginald B Lode and was opened in 1914 by Field Marshall Lord Grenfell (Gosh!).

At the main road, do a dogleg right and then left and follow the lane round left for Dale Farm. This takes you down through some trees — Dale Farm Conservation Area — to a junction and continues straight on uphill for the farm. The drive bears round to the right of the house and continues up the slight hill. At the farm follow the direction of the bridleway signs and bear to the right of the buildings. Just before the last barn follow the bridleway signs which take you along a track to the top of a field. Continue along the left-hand side of a couple of fields, with pleasant views on your left. This next section is probably the most difficult part of the route. Basically, it involves continuing straight on along the side of arable fields, but fortunately with a reasonable track. At the end of the second field, go through a gap on your left and continue straight on along a narrower track on the right-hand side of the next field. The increasingly ill-defined track continues along the left-hand edge of another filed, eventually arriving at a gap on the left and a bridleway sign. Continue on for **Haselbech** along and around the right-hand side of the field, at the end of which you go right and towards a solid track. Go left here towards a little white house and some woods — look out for Haselbech Hall in the distance on the right. Follow the drive until it meets a lane where you go left. This delightful gated road provides a fast descent back down into Cottesbrooke and the start of the route.

The byway past Crockwell Farm (Canons Ashby route)

Canons Ashby

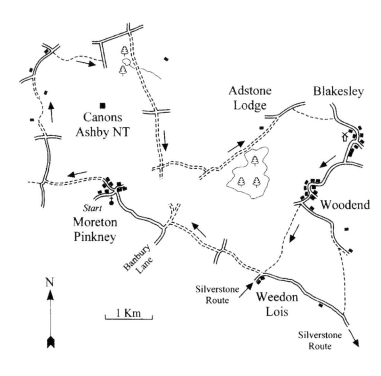

Adstone Lodge

Blakesley

Canons Ashby NT

Start
Moreton Pinkney

Banbury Lane

Woodend

N

1 Km

Silverstone Route

Weedon Lois

Silverstone Route

Canons Ashby

Route Summary
Moreton Pinkney, Crockwell Farm, Woodford Hill, Ashby Gorse, Canons Ashby, Adstone Lodge, Woodend, Weedon Lois, Moreton Pinkney.

Details
Grade — Difficult
Time — 2 1/2 hrs
Distance — 22 km: off road — 16 km
                           on road — 6 km
Terrain — Very gently rolling countryside
Surface — Mostly by-ways, from good to very rutted and soft in wet
Start Grid Reference — SP 575 492
Maps — Northampton and Milton Keynes L152.

Introduction
This route is perhaps best appreciated on a warm sunny day in early summer, after a period of dry weather. During winter the landscape can be a little bleak and the going extremely soft, to say the least!

Although centred around Canons Ashby, the route itself does not visit the pretty hamlet, but a quick detour to see the National Trust house is well worth the effort (if you are in a presentable state!). The name of the village derives from the priory of Augustinian canons that was established here in the 12th century, and the medieval priory church still remains. Canons Ashby is the home of the Dryden family, the most famous member of which was John Dryden, who was the Poet Laureate between 1670-1688. Being a National Trust property the house also has an excellent little tea shop!.

The route is based on the many by-ways that can be found in the area. Most of these are in excellent condition, but unfortunately, those to the south-east of Canons Ashby can be rather churned up, due to the over-enthusiastic use of four-wheel drive vehicles.

Route Description

Start in the village of Moreton Pinkney by The Olde House at Home public house (what better place to start!). If the pub is open, enjoy a quick refreshment, but if not, perhaps this will provide the incentive to complete the route in reasonable time, so as to enable you to return for refreshments at the end. Follow the main road south-west from the pub until you see Brook Street on your right. Follow this down to a ford, over the brook, and continue on a good solid track until you reach a gate at a field. Carry straight on along a good track with the boundary on your right to a second gate, and then down towards some trees. Here you bear right and up to the road by a disused railway bridge. Continue straight on down the small road and eventually up to a junction. Cross over and continue along the track towards Crockwell Farm. Just before the farm, bear right and go up the steep little hill on a good track. At the top, continue past Tile Barn and a small pool, eventually reaching a road. Carry straight on for Preston Capes until you reach a road junction, where you go right and through a gate signposted as a by-way. Follow the sand and gravel track to the bottom of the field where the way divides. Right is a footpath, so go left and up the hill. At the top continue straight on, on a less well-defined green track, past a house and onto the road, where you go left.

Follow the road a short distance to a T-junction and turn right. After about 1/2 km there is another T-junction but you go right, through a gate signed as a by-way and follow the right-hand side of the field on an obvious green track. The track goes past Ashby Gorse with its pool, enters the wood and crosses a concrete drive. Continue straight on, along a good track down the right-hand side of a large field, eventually arriving at a road about 1/2 km east of **Canons Ashby**. This last bit can be very soft. If time allows, take a break and have a look around the old house and grounds, even stop for a cream tea! Otherwise, cross straight over the road and continue on the track, again signed as a by-way (sign — cars not allowed except for loading?). The track is bordered by hedges and is deeply rutted in places, presumably by the over enthusiastic use of four-wheel drive vehicles.

After a while the track opens out into a field and follows down the right-hand side. At the bottom go through a gap, cross over the old railway line and continue up the right-hand side of another arable field. The track improves and at the end of the field go through a bridle gate and onto an excellent unclassified road.

Turn left and follow the road, which is basically a stony track, go over a stream and eventually across a field to some trees. Here you arrive at a clearing, which is really an old junction of by-ways. Turn left (NE) and follow a broad, hedged track (badly rutted in places), bearing right then left, and then continue down the side of a field. Evidence that this is an ancient road is apparent from the old trees that line either side of the by-way. Continue down past woods and between the remains of the old railway line and bridge and on up past a wood. In spring and early summer this wood is a mass of wild flowers and the track itself is adorned with clumps of cowslips. Don't pick the flowers, leave them for others to enjoy! Continue on through a gate and past **Adstone Lodge** to arrive at a road. Go straight on (right) and after c.350 metres you will see a bridleway on the right. Go through the gate and along the right-hand side of a field eventually to arrive at a gate. Go through this, across a short stretch of grazing land to a gate by a road and turn right. Follow the road into **Blakesley** (look out for the old windmill) and go right at the village green, for Woodend. Stop for more refreshments at the Bartholomew Arms, then bear right outside the village, soon to arrive at the village of **Woodend**. Go right in the village and follow the road round (signed for Weston) to arrive at Woodend Green. At this point you can link to the Silverstone route (if your feeling really fit) by going left at the junction and following the lane down towards Green's Park.

At the Woodend Green junction, go left and then immediately right, where there are some green gates (no signpost). Go through these (this is a bridleway) and along the right-hand side of field on a good track to an old barn. Go through a gap and along the right-hand edge of another field to a bridle gate. This next section can be very difficult and it may be necessary to get off and push/carry at this

Canons Ashby

point. Continue straight on, through the gate, by the side of a large arable field and then head straight across and down to the bottom. Here you will see a barbed wire fence with a primitive stile. The worst of this section is now over. Climb over the stile and cross the pasture to a ford with a bridge. Cross the stream and go left around the bottom of a field on a definite track. As you climb up the slight hill the track improves, until eventually you reach a gate by a road junction near **Weedon Lois**. This is the point at which the Silverstone route would rejoin (if you were mad enough to do the detour!).

Go right at the junction and along the tree-lined green lane to Moreton Pinkney. The definite track leaves the trees and continues along the right-hand edge of two fields, to arrive at a gate at a road. Cross over the road and go through a gate following the by-way sign. Continue along the right-hand edge of three fields passing through gates on a less well-defined track, but on grazing land. Eventually you arrive at a gate by some woods, through which you continue on to a clearing, which is a by-way cross-roads. Go left to the road, then right and soon you find yourself back in Moreton Pinkney, in time perhaps for a quick drink!

Banbury Lane (Silverstone route)

Silverstone

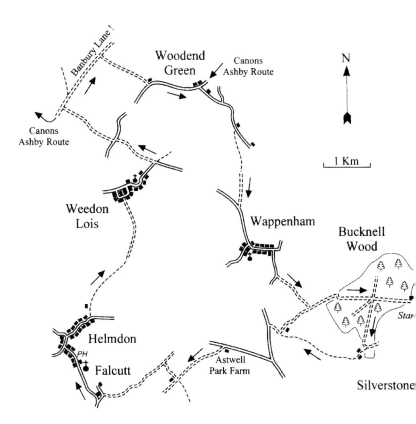

Banbury Lane

Woodend Green

Canons Ashby Route

N

Canons Ashby Route

1 Km

Weedon Lois

Wappenham

Bucknell Wood

Helmdon

PH

Falcutt

Astwell Park Farm

Star

Silverstone

Silverstone

Route Summary
Bucknell Wood, Astwell Park Farm, Falcutt, Helmdon, Weedon Lois, Banbury Lane, Woodend Green, Wappenham, Bucknell Wood.

Details
Grade — Very Difficult
Time — 4 hrs
Distance — 30 km: off road — 21 km
                    on road — 9 km
Terrain — Very gently rolling countryside
Surface — Some good tracks, but some difficult bridleways and by-
            ways, especially in wet.
Start Grid Reference — SP 658 448
Maps — Northampton and Milton Keynes L152.

Introduction
This route starts at the Forest Enterprise Bucknell Wood, just to the north-west of Silverstone. Renowned for its motor-racing circuit, the roads adjacent to Silverstone can get busy on some Sundays. However, our route uses the ancient byways and bridleways that abound in this area, and which are excellent for traffic-free exploration.

Cycling is not allowed on the private tracks in Bucknell Woods, but the woods are traversed by a byway and a bridleway, which makes it an excellent way to start our route. After leaving the woods, our route uses a bridleway that can be tricky in places, and then a combination of country lanes, bridleways and an excellent old county road takes us to Helmdon. A further bridleway continues the route to the very quaint village of Weedon Lois, and at this point the explorer has three possibilities.

If the weather has been very poor, the rider might want to sneak back to the start via the road to Wappenham! Alternatively, those made of stronger stuff might like to savour the little excursion via Banbury Lane, but be warned, wellies (tied on with string!) might be needed. Banbury Lane is an interesting example of an old drove road that ran between Banbury and Northampton and was used by people in years gone by to herd cattle across country to market. The lane was most intensively used in the 17th and 18th centuries, but the development of the railways in the 19th saw a decline in its use. Unfortunately, the most popular use for the lane these days seems to be as a 4 x 4 off-road challenge — you have been warned! A final alternative would be to link this route with the Canons Ashby route, which it slightly overlaps. This extensive route would be ideal for those super-fit individuals who like a different sort of challenge. Whatever your choice, watch out for the byway back into Bucknell Wood!

Route Description

Start at the carpark in Bucknell Wood. You will have noticed that just south of the carpark is a dead straight wide track, which is in fact a byway. Head west along this and enjoy it as not all the byways in these parts are as good! After about 3/4 of a kilometre you come to a major cross-roads of tracks and you go first left, down a grassy track which is a bridleway. This track can be soft in places but, if it is, this is nothing compared to what will follow. Soon you leave the wood via a gate by a pond and, after going through another gate, you bear left for a farmyard. The bridleway turns right, in front of the farm, and just to the right of the barns you will see a gate. After going through this and another gate, aim for a gap in the hedge on the opposite side of the field. Here you will see that the bridleway turns right and you continue down the left-hand side of the field to a small bridle gate. Continue straight on along the edge of the next field and through yet another gate. Thus far the going has been easy, but the bridleway now follows along the left-hand edge of an arable field with a wood on your left. This can be a bit overgrown and rutted in places, but eventually at the end of the field you will discover a small bridle gate that takes you into the wood. After a pleasant ride along a narrow track through the wood, you exit via a gate and cross over a field used for grazing to another gate. Continue on down a narrow field, the going made easier thanks to a sheep track, to arrive at a gate. Cross the next field to another gate and onto the drive (which is also a by-way) of Wappenham Lodge Farm. Carry straight on and you soon come to the road.

At the road go left, and then take the first right. Follow the road and just past **Astwell Park Farm**, there is a bridleway on the left. Follow this excellent wide track for about a kilometre. After a while the track opens out and you will see some trees ahead. Continue on towards these and then turn right and down the track by the house, which up to this point has been hidden. The track descends with a fine view in front, and arrives at a lane. Turn left onto this unmetalled road and enjoy a restful ride into the village of **Falcutt**. At the village continue straight on and up to a road, where you go right for Helmdon. Follow the pretty road down past the church and into **Helmdon**. Stop off for refreshments at the Bell Inn, and then continue down to a junction, where you go right. Bear right again for Wappenham and, just as you are leaving the village, you will see a bridleway on your left.

Follow the bridleway up to a gate and continue on down a definite, but sometimes overgrown track, which crosses an arable field. At the bottom you come to a small bridle gate, after which you bear left and across and down to another bridle gate. Continue along the right-hand edge of the next field and around to a small bridge or, if you're feeling really brave, a soggy looking ford across the stream. The route then continues up the left-hand edge of another arable field on a well-defined track, to arrive at a wide grassy lane with a signpost which looks a bit out of place. Follow this lane for Weedon Lois up and then down to a gate. Continue on down, over a stream and eventually up into the village, by a school. Turn right here, round to the main road, and right again. The road takes you through the village of **Weedon Lois**, which has an interesting collection of houses. Look out for the thatched cottage and just past that, the curious little house with the funny chimney. Follow the road out of the village and, where it goes sharp right, you will see a track signposted 'Green Lane to Moreton Pinkney'. Now, if you're not of a masochistic nature and you have no great love of mud, you might want to continue on round and down to Wappenham. This would be a shame as you would miss what can only be described as the crux of the route. This is also the point at which our route joins the Canons Ashby route for a while.

Follow the tree-lined green lane which soon leaves the trees and continues along the right-hand edge of two fields, to arrive at a gate by a road. Cross over the road and go through a gate following the byway sign. Continue along the right-hand edge of three fields passing through gates on a less well-defined track, but on grazing land. Eventually you arrive at a gate by some woods, through which you continue on to arrive at a clearing, which is a byway junction. This is the infamous **Banbury Lane**.

If you wish to continue on the Canons Ashby route, go left here and then follow the road to Moreton Pinkney. Those who want a bit of fun, however, might like to continue with this route. There is no real way of describing Banbury Lane — it has to be experienced. Images of dense tropical rain forests (after a rainy day) spring to mind. There are several ways this section can be negotiated, and although riding is probably not the best, it can certainly be fun (if you have a warped idea of fun!). At the byway junction turn right and commit yourself. After a kilometre of hell the track opens out into a clearing where you can, thankfully, have a rest. On your right you will see a track, which is another byway. Follow this reasonably well-defined track across an arable field and down to Plumpton Wood. Here it enters the wood and a little bit of hell returns. Battle your way through and eventually you exit the wood and collapse by the side of the road. At the road go left and towards **Woodend Green**.

If you had decided to go off and do the Canons Ashby route, you will rejoin our route at this point. At Woodend Green turn right and follow the lane down towards Green's Park. Watch out for the speed bump just before Cavalilly Cottage, and the bridleway on your right just after. Follow this across an arable field, through a little gate

Bridleway to Weedon Lois

and down to a large gate with a bridleway sign. Continue on down into the valley and through a small plantation and woods. Go over a stream, through another gate and climb up the hill with the track improving as you go. Eventually the excellent track brings you down to the lane, where you go left for **Wappenham**. Follow the road through the village and then turn right for Syresham. Climb the steep little hill and, where the road bears right, go through the gate on your left, which is a byway. Follow the less than distinct track though a few fields until, just past a barn, you join another byway from Wappenham Lodge Farm. Go left, through a gate and towards the woods. After another gate you enter a wide grassy lane which, after wet weather, can be the sting in the tail of the route. Eventually, however, you come to a clearing where you go right, through a gate, and into **Bucknell Wood**. The track bears round to the left and improves and finally takes you back to the start of the route.

Brinklow

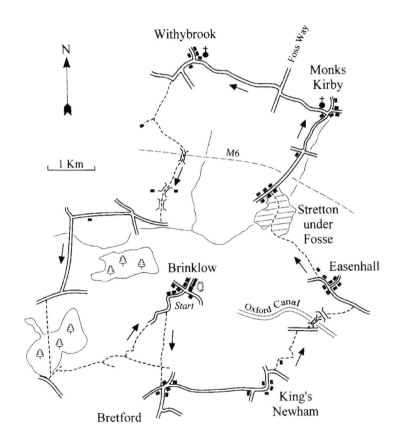

Brinklow

Route Summary
Brinklow, Bretford, King's Newnham, Easenhall, Newbold Revel, Stretton under Fosse, Monks Kirby, Withybrook, Upper Smite Village, Coombe Abbey, Brinklow Heath.

Details
Grade — Very difficult
Time — 3 hr, depends very much on the state of the bridleways!
Distance — 30 Km: off road — 16 Km
                               on road — 14 Km
Terrain — Farm land
Surface — Bridleways along edge of fields and in woods
Start Grid Reference — SP 435 792
Maps — Leicester and Coventry L140

Introduction
This route uses a cluster of bridleways around the village of Brinklow, just 10 km east of Coventry. Horse riding is popular in this area so the tracks are reasonably well defined. Unfortunately, as the land is low lying, in wet weather the tracks can also become extremely chopped up by the horses. This is especially true of the bridleway from Brinklow to Bretford, where there can be some quite impressively muddy puddles. After a period of dry weather, however, the tracks tend to be firmer and less bumpy, with only the occasional splash!

The bridleway from Easenhall to Stretton under Fosse requires a special mention. According to the definitive map, the right of way starts at Farm Lane, goes through the yard of Welkin Farm and over Tumley Hill. The owners of the land, Mr Postlethwaite & Sons at Welkin Farm, have indicated however, that they feel it would be easier for the public to divert slightly by using a path around the edge of the village cricket pitch, which they own, and join the excellent track which leads towards Stretton, and which is eventually joined by the bridleway proper. Signs have been erected to encourage this and the route is well used by the locals. In fact, this private track is much better than the bridleway, but if in any doubt, follow the right of way.

Route Description

The route starts at the main junction in Brinklow. Go right on the Coventry road and almost immediately go left down Heath Lane. Follow the lane as it bears round to the left. Where the road turns sharp right, continue straight on along an unsignposted bridleway between hedges. The track, which is narrow and can be extremely soft in places, rises uphill gently and crosses another bridleway. Continue straight on and down, sharing the track with a muddy stream, to eventually come out by a house and at the main road in the village of **Bretford**. Go left and past The Queens Head pub. Where the main road, which is the Foss Way, turns left you continue straight on for **King's Newnham**. After about 2 km you pass the remains of the old church at Newnham Hall and then the village. The road does a sharp left and rises up hill to a junction, where you go right. As the road further bears right, you continue straight on and along a track marked by a bridleway marker. The track bears left down to some farm buildings, then turns sharp right past the last building (do not be tempted to continue straight on). The track proper is not obvious at first, but is quite passable and eventually, after following around the edges of fields used for grazing, arrives at a lane. Go right and after about 100 m you will see a marked bridleway on the left. Follow this over the Oxford Canal, under the railway line and, where the track forks, go right and along a wooded track, soon arriving at a lane which takes you to the road.

Go left at the road and after less than a kilometre, you arrive at the attractive village of Easenhall. Go past the pub to the village green, bearing right where it is signed 'Bridle Road to Stretton under Fosse'. The right of way goes through the yard of Welkin Farm and continues over the hill (see introduction). However, most locals go left through . a gate, and around the right-hand edge of the village cricket pitch,

eventually arriving at a gate and left onto a superb hard-pack track. This crosses open parkland to some woods and is joined by the bridleway proper. The track continues around the edge of Newbold Revel College and, where it enters the grounds at a gate, you bear left following the bridleway marker. Follow the track across the main drive of the College and continue through a gate and around the edge of the grounds. Soon you come to another drive, where you go left and up to the main road in **Stretton**, by The Union Jack Inn.

At the main road, turn right and pass over the M6. Shortly, the road bears sharp right at a junction, but you continue straight on along a minor road, sign-posted **Monks Kirby**. In the village take the first left by the Denbigh Arms, for Withybrook. Soon you arrive at the **Foss Way** where you do a dog-leg by going right, then left, and continue along the lane to the quaint little village of **Withybrook**.

After perhaps stopping at the pub for refreshments (excellent food!), go south-west along the B4112 for a short distance and, as the road turns left, continue straight on along a lane. Shortly this bears sharp right, but you continue straight on, through a double gate and along a bridleway. The track crosses a field, goes through another bridle gate and now, enclosed by trees, becomes firmer as you climb the hill. At the top you pass through a gate and into a field where, after about 50 m on the left, there is another large gate with a bridleway sign. Follow this grass track along the back of a wood, through two more large gates, and into a field. The bridleway skirts round the right-hand side of the field, through another large gate and again right and around the edge of the field.

Eventually you reach a gap in the far corner of the field, which takes you over a bridge with excellent views of the **M6** motorway (you don't get this kind of thing in the Lakes!). The track then continues down the left-hand side of a field, through a gate on the left, and towards some farm buildings to another gate. After going through this the track descends slightly, past the farm, and out onto a metalled track. Go right, over the railway line, and the Oxford Canal again, then follow the road down to a T-junction.

At the road go right and along to a cross-roads where you go straight across for Coombefields. The road takes you past Peter Hall farm to a junction with a lovely view of the Rolls Royce factory opposite (well, this is the heart of the industrial Midlands, what else do you expect?). This may not be the most stunning section of the route, but it is well worth the effort for what is to follow! Go left and soon you reach another junction where you turn right for Coventry.

After a few hundred metres and opposite the main entrance to Coombe Abbey Countryside Park, you will see an excellent sandy track on your left. This is called Twelve O'clock Ride on the maps, presumably because it runs almost north-south.

Zoom along the track until you reach a gate at the entrance to a wood. Go through the gate and enjoy the ride through the woods, eventually arriving at a lane, where you go left. Near the end of the lane and just before a house, turn right and follow the track which goes around the side of the house. Things can get rather soft in places here, so be prepared to get slightly muddied! After a while you will see a bridleway on the right which leads down to Brandon and, not long after this, there is a fork. Right and straight ahead leads to Bretford, but we bear left along a firm, but narrow tree-lined track. Soon you fork left again, then bear right, and follow the solid track along the edge of a field to a gate. The track becomes metalled and eventually leads back into Brinklow and the completion of the route.

The Priors

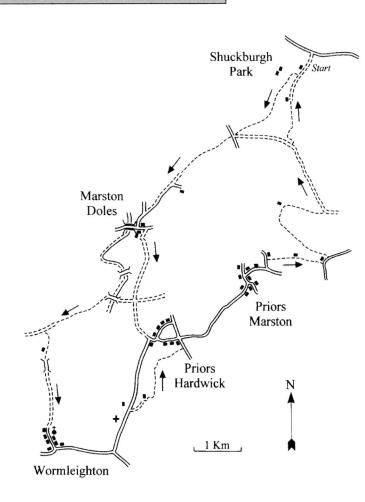

Shuckburgh Park

Start

Marston Doles

Priors Marston

Priors Hardwick

N

1 Km

Wormleighton

The Priors

Route Summary
Shuckburgh, Marston Doles, Wormleighton, Stoneton, Priors
Hardwick, Priors Marston, Shuckburgh.

Details
Grade — Difficult
Time — 3 1/2 hrs
Distance — 30 km: off road — 22 km
                     on road — 8 km
Terrain — Flat with a few bumps.
Surface — Bridleways and tracks across mixed farm land.
Start Grid Reference — SP 503 620
Maps — Stratford-upon-Avon & surrounding area L151.

Introduction
This route is specifically designed for those who do not like hills and
who have a particular liking for field bridleways! As can be seen,
quite a significant part of the route is off-road, with some excellent
tracks, for example, towards Wormleighton and also from Hellidon.
It must be said, however, that bridleways alongside and across fields
are extensively used. In winter, or typical wet summer conditions for
that matter, these tracks can get quite difficult. The fields in this area
are a mixture of grazing and arable, but in most cases definite tracks
are preserved, even where they cross fields. Exceptions to this can be
found on the bridleway before it joins the excellent track into
Wormleighton. However, these are quite short and it is well worth the
battle, if only to enjoy the track which follows.

The route visits several interesting and unspoilt villages, of
particular note is Wormlieghton. This quiet little village has a rather
curious Tower, which is in fact, a gate house to the old manor. Built in
the 1500s by John Spencer, an ancestor of Lady Diana Spencer, most
of the manor was destroyed at the time of the Civil War, and little

more than the tower remains. The parish registers also record connections with another famous person, that of George Washington's family. Priors Hardwick and Priors Marston also deserve a special mention. Both of these fine villages contain many quaint little ironstone cottages, with some good pubs, and are well worth a quick tour.

Since the original version of the route appeared in the Midlands guide it has come to the author's notice that British Waterways do not really allow, for health and safety reasons, cycling along the Oxford canal south of Marston Doles. They are aware that it takes place, but officially it is not allowed. The author has therefore changed the route, and some interesting unclassified roads just to the east of the canal are used instead.

Route Description

The route starts on the main A425 at a little lane just to the east of Shuckburgh Park. If car parking here is not possible, then an alternative start would be in Lower Shuckburgh itself, but this would involve riding on a little over a kilometre of main road. Starting at reference point 503620, take the small lane south until you pass a cottage and track on the right, and continue on down to a gate. Go through this and then immediately right and through another gate, which carries a bridleway marker. Follow an ill-defined track around the right-hand side of the pasture, through a gate and continue on up the field. At the top go through another gate and along the left-hand side of the field on a more defined track. Carry on through another field, now along the right-hand side of a field, contouring around the hill until you arrive at a gate and out onto a road.

Cross over and slightly right to a gate with a bridleway sign, and continue along a track on the left-hand side of the field. This track is, I believe, called Marston Doles Lane. After a second field you arrive at a gate and a rare thing in these parts, a view! If you look to the right you should see Napton on the Hill with its distinctive windmill. Carry on down the hill to a gate, along a green lane, and then along the left-hand side of an arable field. Eventually, after a few more gates, the well-defined track becomes a green lane, which then becomes metalled as it passes Potash Farm, and leads down towards **Marston Doles**. At a junction go left (straight on), soon arriving at a T-junction, where you go left again, but not before having a quick look at the Oxford Canal.

Follow the road towards Priors Marston and very soon you will see, on the right, a lane. Follow this up towards a house, where the wooded lane then bears left. Follow the old county road and then take the track right, which takes you to a bridge over the Oxford Canal and into a field on the other side. This next section can be a little awkward, and could be very difficult in the wet. Cross the field in a general south-westerly direction, aiming for the radio mast in the distance. On the far side of the field you come to a gate, where you continue straight on across the next field along a definite track. Eventually you arrive at an old gate, followed by a short stretch of pasture and another gate. After crossing a further field you come to an overgrown corner, where there is a wooden bridge and a gate which leads into a green lane. Still aiming for the radio mast, continue along the lane for about 100m until it opens out into a field. At this point go left and due south, around the left-hand side of the field, shortly to arrive at a barn. Here you will probably be extremely relieved to find an excellent track and that the most difficult part of the route is now over. Follow the superb track, which climbs very gently up towards **Wormleighton**. This pretty little village has many attractive houses and the rather curious building, The Tower. Soon you arrive at the main road in the village, where you go left.

Follow the road for just over 1 km and the turn left for Priors Hardwick. After about another kilometre and just opposite the site of the medieval village of Stoneton, you will see on the right the drive to Berryhill Farm. Climb the steep little hill, admiring the view as you go, until you arrive at the farm. Go right, through a gate and follow a track around the edge of the field, to the back of the farm. Continue on the track along the left-hand side of a field and down to a line of trees, where you go left. Follow along the right-hand side of the field by the side of the trees, until you reach a gate which leads into an arable field. Things get slightly difficult here, but if you continue on around the left-hand edge of the field, you soon come to a double gate which leads into a pasture. Go right and down to the end of the field, past a pool, to a double gate and onto a green lane. Follow this charming lane, which does a sharp right and leads down to another gate and into another pasture. This is obviously an ancient route as the track continues on down between lines of old oaks and hawthorn. Soon you come to a gate, which is followed by a couple more pastures and eventually leads out onto a lane.

Go left and along the lane, soon to arrive at a cross-roads. Our route goes right here, but it is well worth the effort of a detour through the very pretty village of **Priors Hardwick**, if only to visit the Butcher's Arms for quick refreshments (if you are in a fit state!). In any case, follow the road out of the village for Priors Marston, which is a little over a kilometre away. When you arrive at the village, go left and then first right, for Hellidon. Climb up steeply out of the village and then go left at the top of the hill. Continue along the lane for a short distance, until you see a farm on the right, by the side of which is a track with a bridleway sign. Follow this good dirt track along the side of a couple of fields, eventually arriving at a gate. Continue straight on across a pasture and towards a farm. Follow the bridleway markers past the farm until, where the private drive goes right, you continue on and through a gate into an arable field. Follow along the left-hand edge of this and at the far end, go through a gap in the hedge and out onto a road, where you go left.

In less than 200 metres and just past a house, go left where there is a bridleway sign and follow the excellent track, with pleasant views, along the side of a large golf course. Eventually you come to a gate, after which you continue along the left-hand side of a field and down a tricky little descent. Follow the bridleway sign along the edge of the next field, then turn right and go across the field on a good track towards a barn. Go past this to a gate, through which you turn right, and after passing through another gate, along the bottom of

Oxford Canal at Marston Doles

some woods. This takes you alongside the golf course and after a couple more gates, you come out onto a by-way, where you go left.

Follow this excellent track, which is a pure joy to ride and goes in an almost dead straight line, until finally bearing left. Just around the corner you will see a bridleway sign on the right. Follow this through a gate and along the left-hand side of a field on a reasonable track. After a short distance you will see a gate on the left, with a bridleway marker. Take this and continue along the right-hand side of a field for a couple of hundred metres, to turn right through another gate and then along the side of the next field to a further gate. Continue on through this and across the pasture towards Park Farm, after which you take the track which eventually leads back to the main road at Shuckburgh and the start of the route.

Leicestershire Bike Round

Route Summary
Rothley, Barkby, Baggrave, Tilton on the Hill, Tugby, Stonton Wyville, Foxton, Fleckney, Peatling Magna, Dunton Bassett, Sapcote, Earl Shilton, Desford, Newtown Linford, Rothley.

Details
Grade — Very Severe
Time — Lots!
Distance — 120 km (all distances approx): off road — 70 km
                                          on road — 50 km
Terrain — Everything (except mountains!)
Surface — The whole menu
Start Grid Reference — SK 582 124
Maps — Nottingham and Loughborough L129, Leicester and
       Coventry L140, Kettering, Corby & surrounding area L141.

Introduction
Since the author started researching off-road routes in the Midlands, it became clear that the many routes around Leicester could be linked together to form one super-route. A footpath route, The Leicestershire Round, has been in existence for many years. The route that is presented here is in no way perfect and the author looks forward to hearing of others' suggestions for improvement. A problem with the countryside adjacent to any city is that of major trunk roads and industry. Perhaps the most difficult section was that between Rothley and Barkby at the start of the round. The author has tried to minimise the use of main roads as far as possible and in fact, the section between Barkby and Thorpe Langton to the east of Leicester is almost entirely off-road. Unfortunately, although cycling is allowed at present along the bottom path in Bradgate, it is actually a footpath and this section could not be included in the route. If you decide to have a go at the Leicestershire Bike Route, have fun!

Leicestershire Bike Round - 1

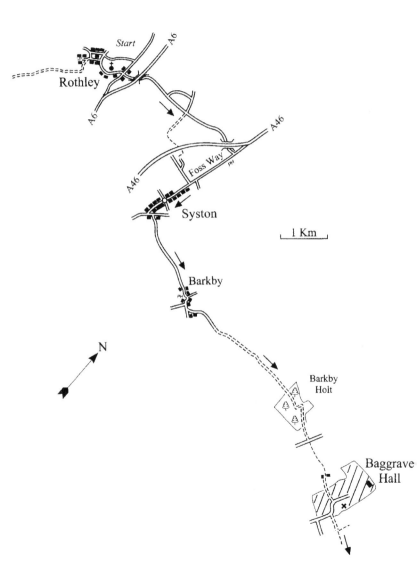

Rothley to Baggrave

The Leicestershire Bike Round starts in the old part of the village of Rothley, by The Bell Inn. At the junction with the road, go right (straight on) and then right at the next junction for Cossington. Follow the road round and up to the traffic lights on the old A6, where you go straight across. Go under the new road and continue on for Syston.

Opposite the second turning for Cossington, go right, by a house and down a gravel track. This takes you past a barn and on a good track, across an arable field. Unfortunately, when you reach the other side the track becomes rather vague, so aim for the fence in the far left-hand corner. Here you will find a stile which, with bike in hand, you leap over! Go under the A46 (mind your head, so push your bike) and then turn right and over an old bridge. Go through a gate, cross the field to another gate, and then over a brook via a couple of bridges. The track then joins Meadow Lane, which eventually takes you to a new road. Go left here and then right at the junction for Barkby. You soon arrive at a little roundabout, where you go left and then first right for Barkby and Beeby. You have finally escaped into the countryside!

Eventually you arrive at the charming village of **Barkby** where you continue on for Beeby. About 100 m past Thorpe Lane, take a small road left, Barkby Holt Lane. Follow the lane on tarmac for over 2 km, when the RUPP becomes a good solid track which heads into some woods. The track does a left turn in the woods by a large tree and then arrives at a T-junction. Turn right, along what is called on the maps Ridgemere Lane, and enjoy a fun ride on an excellent track. This eventually reaches a small bridle gate, through which you exit the wood and continue along the edge of a couple of fields to arrive at a road.

Go through a gate on the opposite side of the road and cross a couple of fields and then along the side of a hedge to arrive at Waterloo Lodge Farm. Continue through the farm and along the drive, which eventually takes you to a road and Baggrave Park.

Leicestershire Bike Round - 2

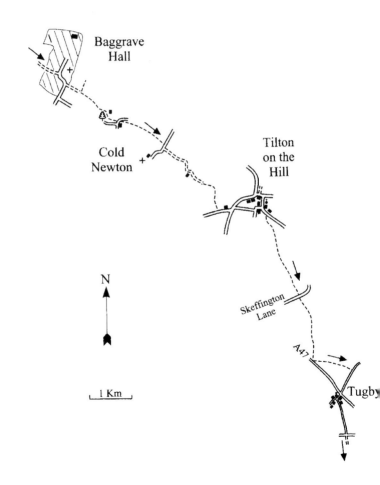

Baggrave Hall

Cold Newton

Tilton on the Hill

Skeffington Lane

A47

Tugby

N

1 Km

Baggrave to Tugby

Continue straight on and where the road bears right, go through a couple of bridle gates and into a lane. Struggle along this to a gate, go straight across the field, through a small bridle gate, across another field, then down a fenced bridleway to the front of Inkerman Lodge. Through some more gates and a coppice brings you out onto a road.

Cross the road and follow the bridleway for **Cold Newton**. Descend to a small bridge, go over a stream and through a gate. Continue over a little hill to another gate and bridge, where you turn right along the bottom of the field and through another gate and up to a road. A little further up the road you will see the track for Hamner's Lodge on the left. Follow this downhill, over a stream and steeply up past the Farm. The track climbs, and enters a large field. Go right at the guide post, up to a gate, and then follow the edge of the field round to the left. Bear left at a gate by some barns, through another gate and out onto Tilton Lane (**Tilton on the Hill**).

Turn left at the road and then left again onto the B6047. Immediately go right for Oxey Farm and down to a T-junction, where you go left, and down to another T-junction. Go right here and soon you will see a bridleway sign on your right. Follow this up the track for Shepherds House. The track descends past some barns and, where it bears left for the house, you go right, through a gate and along the bottom of a field. After going through a little bridle gate and a small field, you continue along the right-hand edge of a large field, round to a bridge. Go over this and then straight up and across an arable field (tricky). After crossing a second arable field you arrive at a lane, which you cross over.

Follow the bridleway across the field up to a bridle gate, and then follow around the left-hand edge of an arable field, down to another gate. Go through this, bear right, cross over a little bridge and go uphill towards a farm. Continue on a gravel track, cross over a lane and across an arable field. After another gate, near the A47, turn left and aim across the arable field for a distant waymarker. Continue on good track for three more fields to arrive at a road, where you go right and up to the junction with the **A47**. Cross over for Tugby.

Tilton on the Hill (Baggrave to Tugby)

Foxton Locks (Tugby to Foxton)

Leicestershire Bike Round - 3

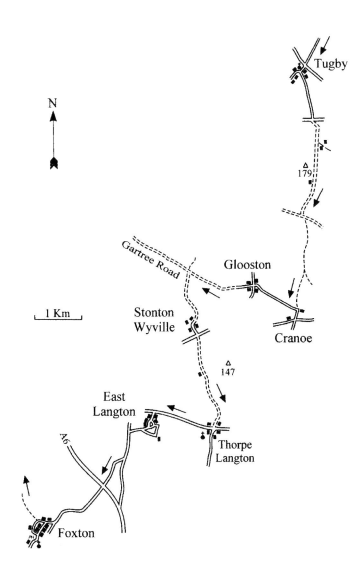

Tugby to Foxton

Follow the road through the village of Tugby and descend a gentle hill to a junction. Go straight ahead where it is signed 'Field road to Keythorpe'. Continue straight on past Keythorpe Hall Farm and along a gravel track up the hill. Go past Keythorpe Lodge Farm and along a good track, passing through a couple of gates. Eventually you arrive at a junction of tracks where you go left, then immediately right, where you see a sign for the Midshires Way.

Follow the bridleway on an excellent track along the right-hand edge of the field until you reach a gate. Now straight on across a large field used for grazing sheep, with fine views to east and west. Eventually you come to a gate on the far side of the field, and continue along the right-hand edge of an arable field on a not such good track. Eventually you arrive at a white gate and into a field used for grazing. Continue down the steep slope and onto the road at **Cranoe**.

Turn right at the road and climb up and then down the hill and into the village of **Glooston**. At the junction go straight on for 'Gartree Road', which takes you into the pretty little village. Bear right past the Old Barn Inn where it says 'Unsuitable for Motor Vehicles'. Follow the green lane, which can be a bit rutted in places, through trees and uphill to a gate. After this the track descends to a crossroads of tracks with a signpost. Go left here for **Stonton Wyville** and down past a farm and into the village.

Cross over at the cross-roads and continue down the track for Thorpe Langton. The track passes some barns, continues along the right-hand side of a field to a gate. Turn left after the gate and follow along the top and down to another gate by a ford. Cross the brook and then continue on up to the village of **Thorpe Langton**.

At the village turn right, follow the road and, after a little over a kilometre, there is a left turn for **East Langton**. Follow the road through the village, past The Bell Inn, fork right and then bear right to arrive at a T-junction, where you go right again. The road takes you up to the B6047, where you go left and then, after the railway bridge, right for Foxton. Continue straight on over the A6 (take care!) and into the village itself.

Leicestershire Bike Round - 4

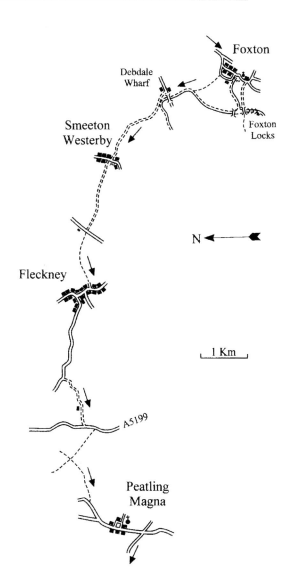

Foxton

Debdale
Wharf

Smeeton
Westerby

Foxton
Locks

N

Fleckney

1 Km

A5199

Peatling
Magna

Foxton to Peatling Magna

In the village bear right all the time and follow a little lane around the back. At a left bend you will see a bridleway on your right. Take this well-defined track along the bottom of a field. Follow around and up to the top of the field, through a gate in the trees and down onto the Grand Union Canal tow-path, where you go north. Soon arrive at **Debdale Wharf** where you leave the canal. Opposite the farm, you will see a track, which is an unclassified county road.

Follow the excellent track, through a gate, downhill and through a couple more gates, eventually to arrive in the village of **Smeeton Westerby**. Go right and then first left. The road soon becomes a gravel track and is a delight to ride. At the road, cross over and continue where there is a bridleway sign.

Follow the bridleway across an arable field, through another bridle gate, down the well-defined track to a bridge over a canal. Continue across the next field, used for grazing, and enter the village of **Fleckney**. Turn right at the end of the road, right again at the silly roundabout, and continue through the village. Turn left at the roundabout for 'Kilby Gated road'. After a couple of kilometres a bridleway crosses the road. You go left, through a gate and along the left-hand edge of the field to another gate. After the next short field, bear right through a gate and then bear left and across a field. Go over a little bridge and on a good track across an arable field and into another field. Keep to the right-hand side, up to a gate, through this and bear left across to another gate on the left of the farm. Go past the farm and down the drive to the main A5199 road.

Turn left at the road and after a few hundred metres you will see a bridleway sign (hidden) on your right. Go through the rusty gate and along the right-hand side of the field used for grazing. Continue through three more fields along the right-hand edge and you come to a bridleway crossroads. Go left and along the right-hand edge of the field. Two more small bridle gates bring you down to a large gate. Continue on good track over a little bridge, bear right to the road, where you go left. Follow the lane and at a junction go left and into the village of Peatling Magna.

Debdale Wharf (Foxton to Peatling Magna)

Two mud-besmattered locals (Peatling Magna to Sapcote)

Leicestershire Bike Round - 5

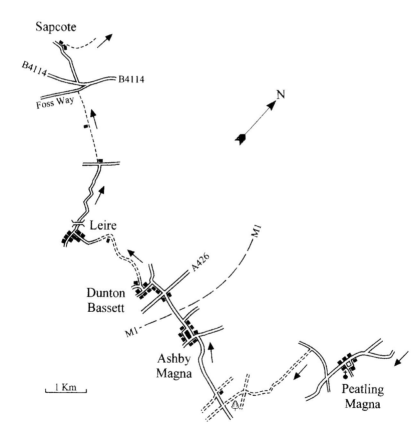

Sapcote

B4114

B4114

Foss Way

N

Leire

A426

M1

Dunton
Bassett

M1

Ashby
Magna

Peatling
Magna

1 Km

Peatling Magna to Sapcote

Go past the Cock Inn, out of the village, and right at the crossroads for Willoughby. At the highest point of the hill you will see a lane on your left marked, 'Unsuitable for Motors'. The old county road soon becomes a gravel track which descends, fords a stream and then climbs up through trees. Follow the track round until at a junction you go left and then bear immediately right, by some woods. Follow the wooded and rutted lane eventually to arrive at a road, where you go right.

Follow the road into **Ashby Magna**, go left at the junction and then right for Dunton Bassett. The road crosses over the M1 and arrives at the A426. Continue straight on for Barwell and then go left for village centre. Follow the road through the village, bear right for Leire and, where the road bears left at the village hall, you go to the right where there is a dead end sign, and down a lane.

Follow the 'Bridle Road to Stemboro Mill', go through a gate and along the right-hand edge of a field, then across the field to another gate with a bridleway sign. Continue along the edge of an arable field along a well-defined path which crosses over into an adjacent field. After going through a gap in the hedge the improved track follows alongside a brook and a large pool. Eventually you arrive at Stemborough Mill, where you go left and follow the lane into the village of **Leire**.

Go right and follow the road out of the village, eventually to arrive at a T-junction. Turn left and then immediately, where there is a bridleway sign, right and up the drive for Sutton Lodge. After going through a couple of gates in the yard (please make sure you close them!), descend on a superb track, over a cattle grid. Continue along the right-hand side of a field and then bear left by some trees and over to a gate, over a little bridge and on up to the road.

This is the **Foss Way** and seems to be all but forgotten due to the adjacent A46. You need to cross this main road to get to Sapcote. Strictly speaking, you should go right for a short distance, left along the A46 and then right for Sapcote, but it is obvious that many people cut through the trees and just cross the main road. Continue on up the road to Sapcote.

Leicestershire Bike Round - 6

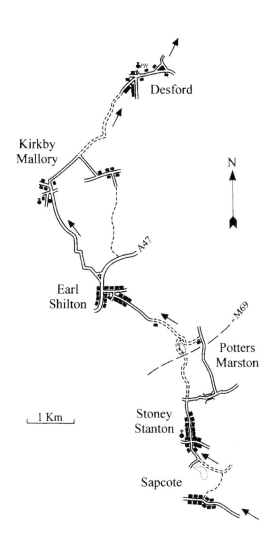

Desford

Kirkby
Mallory

N

A47

Earl
Shilton

M69

Potters
Marston

1 Km

Stoney
Stanton

Sapcote

Sapcote to Desford

As you enter Sapcote you will see a bridleway on your right. After going through a gate, go along a little green lane, past some old quarry workings, and arrive at a gate. Cross a paddock, bearing right, to another gate and onto a dirt track. Go left here, past a farm (and the Stoney Cove diving centre in an old quarry) and down the lane to a road.

Go right (straight on) and up to the crossroads in **Stoney Stanton**. Continue straight over and eventually leave the village. The road bears right, goes over the railway, and you take first left for Potters Marston. Follow the road over the M69 and then turn left by Yennards Farm.

Follow the gravel and pot-holed road, which eventually becomes metalled and is called Mill Lane. This takes you into the village of **Earl Shilton**, where you go right at a junction in front of the church, then left, and then right again at the A47. Follow the road down and out of the village, taking first left for Kirkby Mallory and after a couple of kilometres you arrive at the village.

Alternatively, you could continue a little bit further along the A47 to a bridleway on your left, which will take you to Peckleton, where you go left, then right to rejoin the route. This bridleway, however, follows a stream and is very wooded, so I leave it to your imagination!

As you come into **Kirkby Mallory** along Main Street the road bears to the left, but you go right and down Desford lane. Follow the lane to a sharp right bend at Fairfields and continue straight on along a track signed, 'Unsuitable for Motors'. This excellent track goes over a little ford, eventually becomes metalled, and leads you into the village of Desford.

Leicestershire Bike Round - 7

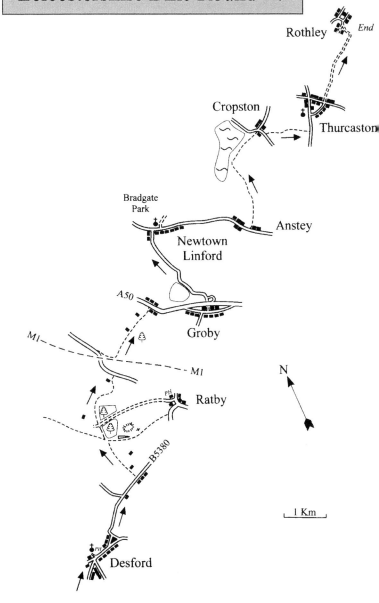

Rothley

End

Thurcaston

Cropston

Anstey

Bradgate Park

Newtown Linford

Groby

A50

M1

M1

Ratby

PH

B5380

N

1 Km

Desford

PH

Desford to Rothley

Turn right in the village and, at the roundabout, straight on for Leicester. Take the first left for Kirby Muxloe. Go left again and, about half a km after Newtown Unthank, you will see a track on the left signed 'Woodland Farm'. Go past a house and, where the track does a sharp right turn for the farm, continue straight on along the left-hand side of the field. After a small gate you descend and arrive at a bridleway junction. Dog-leg left then right, and follow the bridleway up the side of Ratby Burroughs. Cross over a track and ,at the end of the woods, go through a bridle gate and alongside a new plantation. Go past a farm, down a gravel track to a lane, then right, soon to arrive at a road.

Go left at the road, under M1 and very soon you will see a bridleway sign on your right. Follow this through a gate, along parallel to the motorway, and after a couple more gates, turn left by a stream and follow the track which leads to a metalled farm drive. Continue straight on to arrive at the main **A50**. Cross the road (care!) and go right for Leicester. Climb the hill and soon you will see a turning for **Groby**. Go down to a T-junction, where you go right for Groby Pools. The pretty road takes you past the pools and then, after a right bend, descends into **Newtown Linford**. At the junction go right and climb out of the village and down into Anstey.

In the village, look out for a bridleway sign on your left. Go through a small gate, follow the track across a couple of fields, through another small gate, and left down a narrow lane. Cross over a field, and then along the right-hand edge of a larger field. Go over a stream, along the edge of another field, at the end of which you go right. Eventually the track becomes a gravel lane, which takes you into **Cropston**. Go right for Anstey and soon you will see a bridleway on your left. Follow this across a field to an old bridge; cross over and climb up to a road. Go left, down into **Thurcaston**, then turn right up Rectory Lane and down to a T-junction. Cross over, continue down a bridleway which crosses an arable field on a good track. After going over a railway line you enter a delightful tunnel of trees, it passes a golf course, becomes a gravel road, which eventually takes you back to the village of Rothley.

You have now completed the Leicestershire Bike Round!

Appendix

Here are a few useful addresses.

County Councils
Leicestershire County Council, County Hall, Glenfield, LE3 8RJ.

Northants County Council, PO Box 221, John Dryden House, 8-10 The Lakes, Northampton, NN4 7DE

Nottingham County Council, Trent Bridge House, Fox Road, West Bridgeford, Nottingham, NG2 6BJ.

Warwickshire County Council, PO Box 43, Shire Hall, Warwick, CV34 4SX.

Forestry Commission
Northants Forest District, Top Lodge, Fineshade, Nr Corby, Nothants, NN17 3BB.

Sherwood and Lincs. Forest District, Edwinstowe, Mansfield, Nottinghamshire, NG21 9JL.

British Waterways
Marketing and Communications, Willow Grange, Church Road, Watford. WD1 3QA.

Cyclists Touring Club
Cotterell House, 69 Meadrow, Godalming, Surrey, GU7 3HS.